CREATED BY...

CREATED BY...
Inside the Minds
of TV's Top Show Creators

by Steven Priggé

Foreword by Ted Danson

SILMAN-JAMES PRESS   LOS ANGELES

First Edition
10 9 8 7 6 5 4 3

Library of Congress Cataloging-in-Publication Data

Priggé, Steven, 1975-
Created by—inside the minds of TV's top show creators /
by Steven Priggé.—1st ed.
p. cm.   ISBN 1-879505-82-7 (pbk. : alk. paper)
1. Television authorship. 2. Television—Production and direction.
3. Television writers—United States—Interviews. 4. Television producers
and directors—United States—Interviews. I. Title.

PN1992.7.P75 2005
808.2'25—dc22

2005047974

Cover design by Wade Lageose

Printed and bound in the United States of America

Silman-James Press
1181 Angelo Drive
Beverly Hills, CA 90210

For Lina Hansson

The original writer is not one who imitates nobody, but one whom nobody can imitate. — Chateaubriand

Contents

Foreword by Ted Danson

What I really wanted to be when I grew up was a professional basketball player. When I walked out onto the court at Stanford University to try out for freshman basketball, it was instantly clear that I needed to pick a second profession. Acting was the next best thing. It has brought me great joy and continues to every time I get in front of an audience.

I have been blessed as an actor to work with many great writers who had very strong points of view and passion for their work. After Stanford, I was given a classical training as an actor at Carnegie Mellon University. One of the things I walked away with was the belief that "the play is the thing." My job as an actor was, and is, to service the material. Clearly there are some stars who shine all on their own, and some stand-up comics who can and should create their own material. But, I am not one of those. I have always been part of an ensemble that is working together to present a play, and that is why I love half-hour situation comedies so much. It is like being part of a repertory company that puts on a new play every week.

Cheers was my first opportunity to watch the writing process up close. Although I had worked on several films before that, which had been beautifully written, the actual writing process had been completed before I had been hired as an actor. During my 11 years on *Cheers,* I was able to observe a roomful of writers, led by Les and Glen Charles, write and rewrite some of the funniest moments on television. After *Cheers,* I was lucky enough to work with Diane English for a year on *Ink,* and I have just completed five and half years of *Becker,* created by Dave Hackel. I so love these incredibly intelligent and funny men and women who have made me laugh and cry every day for the last 17 years.

Television writing is one of the most rewarding careers in the world, but extremely tough to break into. The author, Steven Priggé, offers the reader a true inside glimpse of the business through the eyes of some of the most brilliant writing minds creating television shows today. Many of the writers/creators interviewed in this book have wonderful pedigrees. Take Tracy Gamble, the creator of *8 Simple Rules for Dating My Teenage Daughter.* He started out writing for the hit show *Newhart.* Tracy Newman and Jonathan Stark, creators of *According to Jim*, got their start writing on *Cheers*. Tom Fontana, creator of *Oz,* began as a writer on the award-winning drama *St. Elsewhere*. And the list goes on. Many of the writers in this book claim they chose TV because it's one of the only mediums in which the writer exercises full control. In theater, the playwright often depends on a strong director. In film, the writer writes the script and a studio then says, "Thank you very much. We'll take that." Then two or three more writers rewrite it, the director adds his or her changes, and, finally, they hire a big star who might also want changes. Don't get me wrong. There's not a lack of respect for writers in film, but the writers certainly don't have the final word. TV show creators do have the final word, and the director essentially works for them. From wardrobe to lights to music—everything is their call. For these reasons, television writing is extremely rewarding, and this is the book that shows you how to do it.

Acknowledgments

This is the place in the book where I thank all of the people who have helped me create *Created by....* If it weren't for these wonderful people, I would have no book to follow this page.

I must first give a very special thanks to all of the television show creators in this book, who were extremely generous, supportive, and so kind to allow me to interview them. It was a sincere honor and pleasure to spend time speaking with each and every one of you. You are all great writers, but more importantly, great people.

I want to thank Ted Danson for his wonderful foreword. He is an intelligent, giving man who has a deep respect for writers. I would also like to thank Dave Hackel for introducing us.

I want to offer my gratitude to Gwen Feldman and Silman-James Press for believing in me and my project. I want to thank my editor, Jim Fox, who did an amazing job.

My deepest appreciation to Lina Hansson, who has always loved and believed in me, no matter the circumstances. Thanks to Alan Priggé, Deanna Priggé, Dana Priggé, Lou Massaia, Keya Morgan, Anthony Edwards, Jeanine Lobell, Jann Yogman, Jules Mignonac, Heather Green and Consuelo Flores.

My appreciation also goes to Alison Mann, Grant Nieporte, Colleen Quinn, Marybeth Sprows, Michael Boretz, Nina Berry, Sam Katchadour, Kristin Campo, Christina Jokanovic, Zuzana Cernik, Heather Hicks, Christi Ayo, Shannon Logan-Torres, Melisa Lomet, Emily Lewis, Eren Celeboglu, Carrie Wick, Laura Fairchild, Justin L. Sternberg, Chris Connor, Renate Kamer, Kathy Eszo, and Ron Hofmann.

Once again, my deepest gratitude to all of the above listed people who shared time in their lives, to help me in mine. I tip my hat to all of you and thank you from the bottom of my heart.

Introduction

The television industry has a never-sated need for writers who can deliver fresh and unique concepts for new television shows that can become all-out audience-acclaimed "hits." The bottom line is that the overall success of a television show falls squarely on the shoulders of the show's creator, since the actors, actresses, and directors follow the script and interpret—rather than create—its theme. Although a show's creator ultimately has a team of writers to support his or her concepts, the show's consistency of theme (as developed through plot, characterization, and dialogue) is largely in the hands of its creator.

There is no questioning the magnitude of a show creator's initial and ongoing contribution. In his or her head alone is the ultimate blueprint responsible for a show's overall impact on an audience. What runs through the minds of these creative geniuses who have turned their ideas into millions and millions of dollars? How did they get their starts? How hard did they struggle to get where they are today? What does their job actually entail?

During my college years, I got an internship to work on the first season of Michael J. Fox's hit ABC-TV sitcom *Spin City*. Eventually, I was hired as a fully salaried assistant and worked directly with the writers and producers for several more seasons. I got to work with the two creators of *Spin City*, Gary David Goldberg and Bill Lawrence. In his late 20s, this was Lawrence's first show-creating effort. He has gone on to further success creating NBC-TV's hit comedy *Scrubs*. On the other hand, Goldberg had a highly successful career prior to *Spin City*, creating, most notably, *Family Ties*. Some of my fondest childhood TV memories were of watching *Family Ties*, with Michael J. Fox in his then break-out role as Alex P. Keaton. When I first heard about the idea of Michael getting back into series television with *Spin City*, I was very excited. After I was hired, I got to learn about creating a show by watching the veteran, Goldberg, and his young, talented partner, Lawrence. It was amazing to see Michael J. Fox acting as brilliantly as ever in his new and unique role as "Deputy Mayor of New York Michael Flaherty."

Working on *Spin City* from its very first season, I got to see first-hand the building of a television show's infrastructure. I saw how a network show is created on an everyday basis. It was amazing to see the evolution of a sitcom script—from its first version that was read aloud at Monday's "table read," through its rehearsals, run-throughs, camera blocking, and, finally, shooting in front of a studio audience. The process was extremely exciting, and I knew I was in the presence of some of the hardest-working and most-talented people in the business, especially the writers. I realized that a special kind of dedication and commitment was required to write and create a top television show. With *Spin City*, like any new show, the network and show's creators wanted to score the best ratings as early as possible. The creators and writers of *Spin City* wrote each script funnier than the last and made me laugh every day. I quickly learned that a job that inspires you to laugh every day is the type of job I wanted. A career that can let you create for a living is a career I desired. However, I also saw that writing and creating television shows was extremely competitive. I would screen hundreds of phone calls a week from agents and aspiring writers who wanted to get in. It made me feel happy to be where I was, as an assistant, but eager to one day get to the "promised land" and become a writer myself.

So, when *Spin City* was cancelled, I realized it was my time to become a television writer. I knew that the competition is tough no matter how many connections you have. So, like any warrior heading into battle, I began to do my own research on how to break into television writing and how to get an agent to represent me. That quest quickly became depressing because of the lack of information available in bookstores for aspiring television writers and fans alike. I wanted to learn how to get started career-wise. I wanted sage advice from the creators/writers/producers of the best shows on television today. I wanted to hear how to overcome the obstacles surrounding television writing from those people who actually did it. Sure, college writing courses teach you about the fundamentals of writing, but what about the "business" of television? What about the harsh realities of self-doubt and failure? What about rising above those factors to create scripts you truly believe in? From my professional curiosity, and as a TV fan, I wanted to know how they came up with the ideas for creating my favorite shows. My inability to find this information anywhere pushed me to embark on writing this book.

I wanted to make *Created by...* as practical and easy to follow as possible. Drawing upon my own experiences of watching *Spin City* being created firsthand, I first broke the subject down into chapters and then sub-topics that I felt were essential in learning how to break into the business and create a television show. Then, I called upon some of the most talented TV creators in the business to shed light on these topics from their own lives and careers. *Created by...* not only tells you how to break in, but also reveals how to write the winning spec script that can get you hired by the very people—the show creators—who read them and can hire you.

I've interviewed the creators of the most exciting and original TV programs on the air—shows like *Will & Grace, Six Feet Under, Joan of Arcadia, Scrubs,*

The Shield, and more. I tackle the pertinent questions on the minds of any aspiring writer (or fan): How did you break into the industry? How did you score an agent? Where did you come up with the idea for your hit show? How do you pitch a network executive? What do you look for when hiring a writer? Plus, many more important questions.

From the show creators' lives that you are about to read about, you'll discover that there's no precise recipe for "making it." Everyone embarked on their own unique journey to reach success. These creators and their shows didn't just arrive on the scene. Through persistence and incredible work ethics, they advanced toward their goals every day. Their personal stories offer the reader an insider's look at the sometimes frustrating, but always exciting, road to success.

The successful show creators interviewed for this book truly stand as examples for aspiring young television show writers and creators everywhere. Time and time again, their stories reflect the fact that the plots for their most successful TV episodes aren't always derived from sheer imagination, but usually originate from events that have occurred in their own lives and those of their immediate families. Even though all of these creators' television shows are different, the one thing that all the creators have in common is that they created shows that they would want to watch on TV themselves.

The Creators

J.J. ABRAMS knew that he wanted a career writing and directing movies and television after his grandfather took him to Universal Studios when he was just eight years old. He started making Super-8 movies during his childhood and has remained on that creative path ever since. During his senior year at Sarah Lawrence College, he teamed up with a friend to write a feature film treatment that became *Taking Care of Business*. He has gone on to write many successful movies, including *Regarding Henry*, starring Harrison Ford, and *Armageddon*, starring Ben Affleck and Bruce Willis. Abrams then turned his attention to television, creating the popular series *Felicity*, starring Keri Russell, and later creating the smash hit *Alias*, starring Jennifer Garner. Abrams is extremely multitalented—writing, directing, producing, and even composing music, including the theme song for *Alias*. He is also the co-creator/executive producer of ABC-TV's acclaimed drama *Lost*.

Writing Credits

Lost — co-creator (2004-present)
Alias — creator (2001-present)
Felicity — creator
Joy Ride (film)
Armageddon (film)
Gone Fishin' (film)
Forever Young (film)
Regarding Henry (film)
Taking Care of Business (film)

J.J. Abrams

Photo courtesy of J.J. Abrams.

ALAN BALL grew up in Marietta, Georgia, and went to college at Florida State University, where he majored in theater. Since Ball had trouble getting work as an actor, he decided to write his own material. His writing talent developed, and he eventually moved to New York City, where he became a noted comedic playwright. Eventually, Ball received an offer to go to L.A. and write for the sitcom *Grace Under Fire.* He took the job and hasn't stopped writing for the screen since that time. Ball's other network television credits include *Oh Grow Up* and *Cybill.* In 1999, Ball received the Academy Award for Best Original Screenplay for his first produced feature-film script, *American Beauty.* Alan Ball is the creator and Executive Producer of *Six Feet Under,* HBO's critically acclaimed drama series, which has received many awards, including the Golden Globe for Best Drama Series. Ball was also awarded an Emmy and a DGA Award for directing the pilot of *Six Feet Under.*

Writing Credits

Six Feet Under — creator (2001-present)
Oh Grow Up — creator
American Beauty (film)
Cybill
Grace Under Fire

Alan Ball

YVETTE LEE BOWSER was born and raised in West Philadelphia, where her creativity surfaced at a young age. As a child, she put on puppet shows, wrote little books, and kept a diary, which she would refer back to for story ideas later in her life. Upon graduating from Stanford University, Bowser got an opportunity to meet one of her idols, Bill Cosby, who was doing a movie on location in nearby Oakland, California. After she told Cosby about her genuine passion to write for television, he set her up with an apprentice job on the first season of *A Different World*. Bowser worked tirelessly at her new job and eventually got hired as a fulltime writer on the show, writing approximately 20 episodes. With the show *Living Single,* starring Queen Latifah and Kim Coles, Bowser became the first African-American woman to create a television show. She has gone on to create other hit shows, such as *For Your Love,* starring Holly Robinson Peete and James Lesure. Bowser is currently the executive producer of her latest hit series, *Half & Half.*

Writing Credits

Half & Half — (2002-present)
For Your Love — creator
Lush Life — creator
Living Single — creator
Hangin' with Mr. Cooper
A Different World

Yvette Lee Bowser

MARK BRAZILL was born and raised in Buffalo, New York. During his youth, he was influenced by author Kurt Vonnegut, comedians Richard Pryor and Lenny Bruce, and filmmaker Woody Allen. In fact, one of Brazill's favorite movies is *Crimes and Misdemeanors*, written and directed by Allen. After moving to La Jolla, California, in 1980, Brazill started hanging out in the Comedy Store to become a writer for a stand-up comic. Then, he decided to take a stab at doing stand-up comedy himself, eventually catching the attention of a top entertainment-management firm, Brillstein-Grey. After Brazill opened for Dennis Miller at the Improv in Cleveland, Miller was so impressed with him that he hired Brazill to write for the first *Dennis Miller Show* in 1990. Brazill went on to write for *In Living Color* and created many TV pilots. After befriending acclaimed TV and film writers Bonnie and Terry Turner, Brazill was hired to write on their hit show *3rd Rock from the Sun* starring John Lithgow. Then, with the Turners, Brazill created *That '70s Show*, which became a huge hit and is currently as popular as ever.

Writing Credits

That '70s Show — co-creator (1998-present)
Mr. Rhodes — creator
3rd Rock from the Sun
In Living Color
The Dennis Miller Show

Mark Brazill

Photo courtesy of Mark Brazill.

Even as a child, **ILENE CHAIKEN** had a creative writing streak. In her suburban Philadephia elementary school, she was the official school poet. However, after attending the Rhode Island School of Design and Brown University, Chaiken decided to become a television executive. She went on to work as an executive for such top entertainment moguls as Aaron Spelling and Quincy Jones. But her desire to write was always with her. During a 1991 Christmas vacation in Telluride, Colorado, Chaiken wrote a feature film script entitled *Esme's Posse*, which helped her get an agent. She went on to write the motion picture *Barb Wire,* starring Pamela Anderson. Chaiken then wrote a film for Showtime called *Dirty Pictures*, which won the Golden Globe. In 2004, Ilene Chaiken created the ground-breaking show *The L Word*, based on her real life and the lives of her friends around her. *The L Word*, which airs on Showtime, was an instant hit, amassing critical and commercial success.

Writing Credits

The L Word — creator (2004-present)
Damaged Care (TV movie)
Dirty Pictures (TV movie)
Barb Wire (film)

Ilene Chaiken

Photo courtesy of Ilene Chaiken.

LARRY DAVID is one of the most successful writers in the history of television. Born and raised in Brooklyn, New York, Larry David started his career on-stage performing stand-up comedy in some of New York City's top venues. He was discovered by producers at the famous comedy club Catch a Rising Star and cast in the short-lived ABC-TV sketch comedy show *Fridays*. David went on to write for *Saturday Night Live* during the 1984-85 season and became frustrated when only one of his sketches was put on-air. In fact, he quit his writing job at *Saturday Night Live* on a Friday, only to return to work on the show the following Monday, pretending he never quit. Sounds familiar? That became the basis of a classic *Seinfeld* episode in which George Costanza quits his job but returns to the Monday-morning staff meeting as if it had all been a big joke. In 1990, David co-created (with Jerry Seinfeld) the mega-hit sitcom *Seinfeld*. David wrote for that series from 1990 through 1996 and returned to write the series finale in 1998. David was nominated for seven Emmy Awards for his writing on *Seinfeld* and won the Outstanding Individual Achievement in Writing in a Comedy Series Emmy in 1993 for the episode "The Contest." That same year, he also shared an Outstanding Comedy Series Emmy. He also received two Writers Guild Awards for *Seinfeld* episodes: one for "The Contest" and one for "Mango." In 1999, David wrote and starred in *Larry David: Curb Your Enthusiasm*, a one-hour documentary special for HBO that spawned the critically acclaimed HBO series *Curb Your Enthusiasm*, which is currently heading into its fifth season.

Writing Credits

Curb Your Enthusiasm — creator (2000-present)
Seinfeld — co-creator
Sour Grapes (film)
Saturday Night Live
Fridays

Larry David

Photo courtesy of HBO. Photo taken by Ron Batzdorff.

Born and raised in Buffalo, New York, **Tom Fontana** had a creative spark inside of him from an early age. After graduating college, he became a stage manager at the Studio Arena Theatre in Buffalo, but he was busy writing on the side. While working in a summer stock theater in Williamstown, New York, Fontana met television director/producer Bruce Paltrow. Eventually, Paltrow asked Fontana if he wanted to come out to L.A. and write an episode of his new medical drama, *St. Elsewhere*. Fontana went out to L.A. and wrote the episode. Afterwards, he was hired by Paltrow to be one of the full-time writers. He stayed with *St. Elsewhere* for many seasons, eventually becoming a producer on the show. Fontana has gone on to big success executive-producing and writing the hit show *Homicide: Life on the Street* and creating the acclaimed HBO drama *Oz*. Tom Fontana and Barry Levinson, under the banner of The Levinson/Fontana Company, have numerous projects in production and development.

Writing Credits

The Jury — creator
Strip Search (TV movie)
Judas & Jesus (TV movie)
The Beat — creator
Firehouse
Oz — creator
Homicide: Life on the Street
Tattingers
The Fourth Wiseman (TV movie)
St. Elsewhere

Tom Fontana

Photo courtesy of Tom Fontana.

TRACY GAMBLE dreamed of becoming a television writer since he was a child. In the neighborhood he grew up in lived a writer for *My Three Sons*, George Tibbles, and all of the kids in the neighborhood, including Tracy, worshipped him. Gamble has made his childhood dream come true, successfully writing sitcoms for 20 years. He started his writing career on the hit show *Newhart* and has gone on to write and produce such other top shows as *227*, *My Two Dads*, *The Golden Girls*, and *According to Jim*. He created ABC-TV's hit *8 Simple Rules for Dating My Teenage Daughter*, which starred the late John Ritter. Gamble bases many of the storylines for *8 Simple Rules* on the experiences of his real-life family, his wife and three kids. The children of his television family are actually named after his very own children—Rory, Kerry, and Bridget.

Writing Credits

8 Simple Rules for Dating My Teenage Daughter — creator (2002-present)
According to Jim
The Geena Davis Show
Hitz
Clueless
Hudson Street
Home Improvement
My Two Dads
Married... with Children
227
The Golden Girls
Newhart

Tracy Gamble

Photo courtesy of Tracy Gamble.

DAVE HACKEL knew he wanted to work in television from a very young age. After he graduated from college, he worked at a local television station in Columbus, Ohio. When that job ended, he moved to Los Angeles, where he ended up working for a product-placement advertising agency, placing products on TV game shows and talk shows. Then, he decided to make the transition into writing and got an opportunity to write a freelance episode for a show called *Fish*, starring Abe Vigoda. Hackel has gone on to write for many classic television shows like *9 to 5*, *Dear John*, and *Wings*. The first show that Hackel created was called *The Pursuit of Happiness*. In 1998, Hackel created the highly popular CBS-TV sitcom *Becker*, starring Ted Danson. On the air for close to six years, *Becker* amassed solid ratings and critical success.

Writing Credits

Becker — creator
The Pursuit of Happiness — creator
Frasier
Wings
Dear John
9 to 5

Dave Hackel

As a child growing up in Chatham, Virginia, **BARBARA HALL** developed an early interest in writing. She often collaborated on stories with her older sister, knowing by the age of eight the career path that lay ahead. Two days after graduating from James Madison University, Hall moved to Los Angeles. On the West Coast, she wrote her first novel, *Skeeball and the Secret of the Universe*, which got the attention of an agent and TV producer Gary David Goldberg. Hall sold her first sitcom story to *Family Ties* and was soon hired as a comedy writer for *Newhart*. Disliking the roundtable format of comedy writing, Hall switched to television drama. She honed her chops in the shadow of Joshua Brand and John Falsey, serving as story editor of *A Year in the Life* before spending a season as co-producer of *Moonlighting* and later as producer of *Anything but Love*. She went on to write for the hit shows *I'll Fly Away, ER, Northern Exposure*, and *Chicago Hope*. In 1999, Hall was tapped to executive-produce *Judging Amy*. Most recently, she created the new hit CBS drama *Joan of Arcadia*. Hall is a true Renaissance woman in Hollywood, because not only does she write books, television, and poetry, but she is in a band called The Enablers, which is currently releasing its second CD.

Writing Credits

Joan of Arcadia — creator (2003-present)
Judging Amy — (1999-present)
Chicago Hope
Northern Exposure
I'll Fly Away
Anything but Love
Moonlighting
A Year in the Life
Newhart

Barbara Hall

Photo courtesy of Barbara Hall.

BRENDA HAMPTON grew up in Atlanta, Georgia, and graduated from the University of Georgia. As a writer, she has had a diverse early career: a tech writer for the U.S. Navy, a corporate newsletter writer, and a stand-up comedy writer for such talents as Roseanne Barr (when Hampton was a joke writer on the stand-up circuit). Hampton got her first job as a TV writer on the show *Sister Kate* and went on to write for such hit comedies as *Blossom* and *Mad About You*. Hampton broke into the hour-long format in 1996 when she created *7th Heaven*, which is produced by Aaron Spelling. The show is still on the air, enjoying continued commercial and critical success. Her latest hit show is *Fat Actress*, starring the talented Kirstie Alley.

Writing Credits

Fat Actress — co-creator (2005-present)
7th Heaven — creator (1996-present)
Safe Harbor — creator
The Love Boat: The Next Wave
Mad About You
Daddy's Girls — creator
The John Larroquette Show
Blossom
Lenny
Sister Kate

Brenda Hampton

Photo courtesy of Brenda Hampton.

While growing up, **BILL LAWRENCE** was a creative writer who wrote for his high-school literary magazine. Following college graduation from William & Mary, Lawrence set his sights on writing for television and moved to Los Angeles. After writing spec scripts, doing the necessary networking, and eventually scoring an agent, Lawrence got staffed as a writer on a TV show, ironically entitled *Billy*. Unfortunately, it only lasted for 13 episodes. Lawrence continued to persevere as he got hired to write on such popular shows as *Boy Meets World, The Nanny*, and the hit comedy *Friends*. Eventually, Lawrence connected with television writing/producing veteran Gary David Goldberg, who created the classic hit comedy *Family Ties*. Goldberg and Lawrence teamed up and created the hit ABC-TV comedy *Spin City*, starring Michael J. Fox. Most recently, Lawrence created the highly successful NBC-TV sitcom *Scrubs*.

Writing Credits

Scrubs — creator (2001-present)
Clone High
Spin City — co-creator
Friends
The Nanny
Boy Meets World
Billy

Bill Lawrence

Photo courtesy of Bill Lawrence.

DENNIS LEONI is Mexican-American and grew up in Tucson, Arizona. He had no original ambitions to become a writer, but did have an interest in acting. He started his career as a stuntman in such films as *Another Man, Another Chance*, starring James Caan, and in such television shows as *Hawaii Five-O*. On *Hawaii Five-O*, he also worked behind the camera, first as a production assistant, then as an assistant director. After his long exposure to the weekly scripts of *Hawaii Five-O*, Leoni decided to take a stab at writing. He moved with his wife from Hawaii to L.A. with only $3,000 in his pocket and a dream to sell his two-hour TV pilot, *Alexandro*. Although Leoni didn't sell it, the well-written script got him an agent, and he was on his way. He has gone on to write for such shows as *Hull High*, *Covington Cross*, and *McKenna*. In 2000, Leoni created the highly acclaimed Latino drama *Resurrection Blvd.* for Showtime. He currently has several projects in the works, including a feature film script.

Writing Credits

Resurrection Blvd. — creator
McKenna
Covington Cross
Hull High

Dennis Leoni

The friendship of **MAX MUTCHNICK** and **DAVID KOHAN** dates back to their childhood, growing up together in California. After college, they decided to join forces as writing partners. Following some lean years, they got hired as writers on *The Dennis Miller Show*. Mutchnick and Kohan then decided they would attempt to create their own sitcom. They were successful in creating their first show, *Boston Common*. However, it was their next show, *Will & Grace*, that would take them to a whole new level of success. For their work on *Will & Grace*, Mutchnick and Kohan have been honored with an Emmy Award for Outstanding Comedy Series, a People's Choice Award (Favorite New Comedy), four Golden Globe nominations (Best Comedy Series), four GLAAD Media Awards (Outstanding TV Comedy Series), and many more. They also created the popular TV series *Good Morning, Miami*. Mutchnick and Kohan are one of the most successful writing teams in television history.

Writing Credits

Will & Grace — creators (1998-present)
Good Morning, Miami — creators
Boston Common — creators
Hearts Afire
Evening Shade
The Dennis Miller Show

Max Mutchnick and David Kohan

David Kohan (left) and Max Mutchnick (right)

TRACY NEWMAN and **JONATHAN STARK** first met as members of The Groundlings, a noted comedy and improv troupe in Los Angeles. They both had diverse careers before their meeting—Tracy as an actress and singer who performed twice on *The Tonight Show* and Jonathan as an actor who appeared in such films as *Fright Night* and *Project X*. They decided to join forces as a writing team and were eventually hired by executive producers Bill and Cherie Steinkellner to write on the hit sitcom *Cheers*. Newman and Stark have gone on to write and produce *The Nanny, Hiller and Diller*, and *Ellen*. They won an Emmy Award for writing the landmark "Coming Out" episode on *Ellen*. Most recently, they created the successful ABC-TV sitcom *According to Jim,* starring James Belushi.

Writing Credits

According to Jim — creators (2001-present)
Hiller and Diller
Ellen
The Nanny
Cheers

Tracy Newman & Jonathan Stark

Photo courtesy of Tracy Newman and Jonathan Stark.

SHAWN RYAN has been writing since his youth. One of his plays won the American College Theater Festival's Best Original Play prize for the New England region and Best Comedy prize for the United States. Because of that play's acclaim, Ryan was brought to Los Angeles to spend a few weeks in the writers' room of the show *My Two Dads* to see how it operated. That experience inspired Ryan immensely. He went on to write for top-rated shows *Nash Bridges* and *Angel*. In 2002, Ryan created *The Shield*. From its modest launch as a little show on a then-unknown network, FX, and featuring a lead role that no "name" actor wanted to read for, *The Shield* has gone on to win critical acclaim and a Golden Globe for Best Television Drama Series. Its lead actor, Michael Chiklis, who plays Vic Mackey on the show, won an Emmy Award for Best Actor in a Drama Series. With *The Shield*, Ryan has not only created a critic's favorite, but an audience favorite as well.

Writing Credits

The Shield — creator (2002-present)
Angel
Nash Bridges
Life with Louie

Shawn Ryan

JOSH SCHWARTZ wanted to be a writer ever since he won an essay-writing contest at sleepaway camp when he was seven years old. Schwartz went on to attend USC's undergraduate screenwriting program. During his sophomore year, he wrote a script entitled *Providence*. Then, during his junior year at USC, the script was bought by Columbia/Sony Pictures. Schwartz switched to TV when he sold a one-hour drama pilot called *Brookfield* to ABC/Touchstone. Schwartz went on to create the TV show *Wall to Wall Records*. However, that show never went to series. His next effort, *The O.C.*, which did go to series, has become a huge success. Critics have hailed *The O.C.* as one of the best drama series to hit television screens in a long time. Schwartz is not only busy with the writing of the show, he also takes pride in helping select the music for this highly popular program.

Writing Credits

The O.C. — creator (2003-present)
The Joe Bonilla Show
Wall to Wall Records — creator
Brookfield — creator
Providence (film)

Josh Schwartz

Photo courtesy of Josh Schwartz.

AMY SHERMAN-PALLADINO has emerged as a true force in television writing and producing. After graduating from college, she set her sights on writing for television. At only 23 years old, she got her first writing job on the hit network comedy *Roseanne*. After several years on *Roseanne*, Palladino went on to write and produce the series *Veronica's Closet*. Eventually, she pitched The WB Network with her idea about a 32-year-old single mom and her 16-year-old daughter, who behave more like friends than mother and daughter. That idea became Palladino's hit show, *Gilmore Girls*. One of Palladino's encouraging statements about her dedication to the craft of writing says it all: "The minute I stop caring about the quality of my writing, I've got to quit this business."

Writing Credits

Gilmore Girls — creator (2000-present)
Over the Top
Veronica's Closet
Love and Marriage
Roseanne

Amy Sherman-Palladino

JOSS WHEDON is a third-generation television writer. His grandfather wrote for such TV classics as *Leave It to Beaver* and *The Donna Reed Show,* while his father wrote for the popular sitcoms *Alice* and *Benson.* After graduating from Wesleyan University with a degree in film studies, Whedon moved to Los Angeles, where he was hired as a staff writer on the hit show *Roseanne.* He then wrote for the NBC-TV series *Parenthood.* He went on to create the cult television hits *Buffy the Vampire Slayer* and the show's highly successful spin-off, *Angel.* Whedon was nominated for an Emmy Award in 2000 for Outstanding Writing in a Drama Series for the episode of *Buffy* entitled "Hush." This unique episode featured an innovative 28 minutes without dialogue. Whedon also composes music for many of his productions.

Writing Credits

Firefly — creator
Angel — creator
Titan A.E. (film)
Alien: Resurrection (film)
Buffy the Vampire Slayer — creator
Toy Story (film)
Buffy the Vampire Slayer (film)
Parenthood
Roseanne

Joss Whedon

Photo courtesy of Joss Whedon.

Beginnings

Early TV Influences

DAVE HACKEL: Somewhat embarrassingly, I'm having a little trouble thinking of a program I *didn't* watch when I was growing up. During the fifties, there were a plethora of family shows of the *Father Knows Best* variety, and I watched them all. *Sgt. Bilko* was one of the first workplace shows I remember—albeit a bit twisted, Phil Silvers' version of a workplace. I suppose, like most TV writers, *The Dick Van Dyke Show* was not to be missed. We all, I think, wanted to be Rob Petrie. *All in the Family* was appointment television, as it was the first television show to turn what you could and couldn't talk about on its ear. *The Fugitive* wasn't to be missed—the hunt for the one-armed man was a national obsession. Then the craftsmanship and humor of *The Mary Tyler Moore Show, Bob Newhart,* and *M*A*S*H* quickly made them favorites as well. As I got older I was drawn to *Taxi* and *Cheers* because they were both funny and very smartly written.

MAX MUTCHNICK: From my early childhood, the only sitcom that stands out for me is *The Odd Couple.* I thought it was really funny. It wasn't until I got older that I took notice of good writing on television shows that I was watching. I thought *Roseanne* and *Hot L Baltimore* were written very well. At the beginning of its run, *Home Improvement* was also enjoyable. I would have to say that I got my true taste of television comedy from one source, and that comedic source has lasted for me for the last 20 years—David Letterman. For as much as I am in television and a part of this business, David Letterman has been a standard for me of what I think is funny. He has taught me a great deal.

LARRY DAVID: My favorite show was *Sgt. Bilko,* starring Phil Silvers. I think I liked it because the worst characteristics of *Sgt. Bilko* were revealed to the audience in an always-humorous way. He was conniving and self-centered, but you just loved him, anyway. I never missed that show as a child and got all the humor at a very young age. Oh, and did I mention he was bald?

MARK BRAZILL: When I was a little kid, I loved watching *Batman.* Later, when I was growing up, I enjoyed watching *Monty Python* and *All in the Family.* I also felt *Roseanne* was a really smart and funny show. I liked those family, blue-collar, 30-minute sitcoms because they related most to my life at that time. I grew up in Buffalo, New York, where there were four kids in my family. My father worked at a dog food factory and my mother worked as an assistant to a president of a steel factory. Even though they did not work in creative fields,

I do remember that my family was extremely funny. My father always had a great sense of humor with a bright, creative mind.

BRENDA HAMPTON: I grew up in the 1950s, and my father was a TV repairman. So, my household was filled with television sets. This was back in the day when every television had tubes. Sometimes, there were a dozen television sets in the house at one time and sometimes none. I loved to watch *Leave It to Beaver, Father Knows Best, The Donna Reed Show*, and *The Andy Griffith Show*. Later, I grew to love *The Mary Tyler Moore Show* and *The Bob Newhart Show*. Those were the kinds of comedic shows I liked the most.

SHAWN RYAN: I was born in 1966 and, as a result, I was a hostage of those late-1970s' hit ABC sitcoms like *Happy Days* and *Laverne & Shirley*. Then, as I got to be a teenager, I think my tastes got a tad more sophisticated as I tuned in to *Taxi* and *M*A*S*H*. As a child, I watched more sitcoms than dramas. Right now, I think we are in a golden age of drama. When I was a kid, it was completely reversed.

BARBARA HALL: I did watch television growing up, but I actually grew up as a fanatical reader. All of my early interest in writing came from that. I was a complete bookworm. Eventually, my interest in Joan of Arc was derived from books, not movies. When I was a teenager, I discovered television to a certain degree. *The White Shadow* was the first show I watched and paid attention to. I also enjoyed *The Bob Newhart Show* and *The Mary Tyler Moore Show* and that whole MTM [Mary Tyler Moore Productions] lineup, which I was a fan of. It was the heyday of MTM. In terms of noticing dramas that were different and interesting to me, I liked the show *Family*, which was sort of breaking away from traditional family television. It was *Hill Street Blues* that completely captivated me and made me want to write for television. I just had never seen anything like it. It was literary and diverse and it was not a single-lead show. It was an ensemble drama, and I had not seen anything like that. It was great, great storytelling. I was in college at the time. I was an English major, concentrating on poetry. So, I was a snob. [Laughing] I wasn't going to dirty my hands writing for TV, let alone dirty my hands watching it. But, I saw *Hill Street Blues* and it completely changed my mind as far as what television truly was.

JOSS WHEDON: I was a big PBS kid. I loved shows like *Masterpiece Theatre, Upstairs, Downstairs, Love for Lydia, Jenny*. I watched them all. Of course, *Monty Python* was a favorite when I was younger. The shows that I genuinely got attached to happened later on in life. I loved *Hill Street Blues, Wiseguy*, and *My So-Called Life,* because those shows hit me right where I live, creatively. However, it was the continuing type of drama shows that really sucked the audience in that made the biggest impression on me. There were also television shows that made me laugh and ones that were exciting too. I also liked *Columbo* and *Kojak*.

TRACY GAMBLE: The television show *Fury*, which was about a ranch family and its horse, really affected me in my youth. I also loved *Ozzie & Harriet* and *My Three Sons*. Wow, I'm really dating myself here. [Laughing] Those shows had a real impact on me. In the neighborhood where I grew up, there was a writer for *My Three Sons* by the name of George Tibbles. All of the kids in the neighborhood worshipped him. To pay homage to the kids in our neighborhood, he would name children in the classroom scenes after us. His son, Doug Tibbles, wrote for *The Munsters*, and all of the kids thought he was the coolest guy around. I think that's where I first got my inspiration to write for television.

YVETTE LEE BOWSER: I grew up with television shows like *Happy Days* and *Laverne & Shirley* and with *The Cosby Show* in later years. *The Cosby Show* kind of demonstrated to me that there was room in the television universe to show that African-Americans were not a monolith. There we were on the same level as the Caucasian families on other shows. Prior to that, we were primarily depicted as broke and trying to dig ourselves out of a hole through shows like *Sanford and Son, Good Times, 227*, and so on. So, *The Cosby Show* gave us hope, especially for those of us who were not from that kind of affluent, cohesive family but aspired to have that kind of life for ourselves. *The Cosby Show* was a genuine inspiration. But, I never really thought about writing for television as a career. Being African-American and female, and hailing from West Philadelphia, I didn't know that option was available to me. I just watched television purely for enjoyment. I was never studying it or dreaming of it as a way of making money and having a career. Most people who watch television do not think about the behind-the-scenes. When I was growing up, I didn't know the names of any television writers or even what that job entailed.

ALAN BALL: I'm not sure what the very first TV shows were that I watched, but I know I loved *Lost in Space* and *Mission: Impossible*. As I got older, it was *The Mary Tyler Moore Show, The Bob Newhart Show*, and *The Carol Burnett Show*— that whole CBS Saturday night lineup. That stayed the same, until I got old enough to drive. Then, I gave up staying home on Saturday nights to watch television. [Laughing]

AMY SHERMAN-PALLADINO: My first TV addiction was *Little House on the Prairie*. Then, I got into all the Norman Lear shows, like *All in the Family* and *Good Times*. However, when John Amos left that show, I stopped watching. Later, I loved *Taxi* and *M*A*S*H*.

Tom Fontana: While I was growing up, to say that I watched a lot of television would be an understatement. *The Twilight Zone* was something that I never missed as a kid. I remember from a drama point of view that I enjoyed *The Defenders* and *Naked City*, two really hard-hitting dramas of the time. As years went by, I loved *All in the Family*. The show *Lou Grant* was great because it dealt with issues. They didn't back away from controversial stuff. One of the reasons why I do the type of television I do is because I have seen all the kinds of versions of it, ranging from the easy, cheap route to the episodes of substance on shows like *The Defenders*, *Naked City*, and *Lou Grant*. On these shows you were totally stunned by the truth that was revealed to you in such a short amount of time.

Dennis Leoni: I grew up in Tucson, Arizona. My grandmother Paula was a Mexican-American woman who loved Westerns. My grandmother and I would watch *Gunsmoke, Bonanza, The Rifleman*, and *The Lone Ranger*—all the great Western TV shows. I really got my love for television from my grandmother because I would sit and watch with her. She would root for the good guys and actually verbally warn them about the bad guys sneaking up on them. I think about it today because I would love to bring back both of my grandparents to our set and show them that there is a writer who actually writes the dialogue. I don't think they ever understood that. My grandparents knew it was a play, but I think they thought the actors made it up as they went along. Anyway, I have always been in love with Westerns.

Bill Lawrence: When I was a kid, I was sort of a pop-culture freak. I was all about movies, plays, and TV shows. My parents didn't just put me in front of the TV, but they could tell that I liked it enough that they used it as a motivational tool. For instance, one of the basic motivating techniques was that I was only allowed to watch TV when I was done with my homework. Across the board, I was always a huge fan of television shows like *M*A*S*H, All in the Family, Happy Days,* the old *Dick Van Dyke Show*, and *The Mary Tyler Moore Show*. Because I was really into basketball when I was younger, I was a huge fan of *The White Shadow*, which was an hour-long "dramedy" [a drama with comedic elements].

Josh Schwartz: I was really into *Family Ties, The Cosby Show, Growing Pains, Cheers*, and *Alf* when I was younger. So, I guess at the top of my list were a lot of those family genre sitcoms. The show *Seinfeld* had the biggest influence on me and was the reason I pursued writing for television as a career. I thought the show was absolutely amazing. I recall never really watching dramas. Our show, *The O.C.*, keeps getting compared to *90210,* but I never even watched that show. It was on everyone's radar in my high school, especially the girls'. However, I never got into it. Looking back, the only drama that I thought was cool, and if I was allowed to stay up late enough to watch it, was *Miami Vice*.

JONATHAN STARK: Growing up, I really liked *Captain Kangaroo, I Love Lucy, I Dream of Jeannie*, and *Howdy Doody*. I also loved *The Monkees. The Andy Griffith Show* was phenomenal. I don't think there has ever been a better show than that. In my office, I actually have signed pictures of Don Knotts, and they're very special to me.

Motivation from Family

J.J. ABRAMS: My father used to sell commercial time for CBS-TV and became a television movie producer. My mother is an author and lawyer and has also produced some TV movies. When my father was at Paramount Studios, I got to wander around and watch them make hit shows like *Happy Days*, *Mork & Mindy*, and *Laverne & Shirley*. That was always a kick because those were the television shows of my generation, having been born in 1966. My grandfather took me to Universal Studios when I was eight years old and it blew my mind. It galvanized the dream for me of writing and directing for film and television. I started making Super-8 movies and just kept going at it ever since.

JOSS WHEDON: My entire family was very creative, theatrical, and artistic. My mother directed and starred in a lot of theater when I was a kid. All of my father's friends were comedy writers. We also knew many poets and musicians. As children, we all knew that we could never be able hold real jobs. [Laughing] I have two older brothers, two younger half-brothers, and a stepsister, and all of them actually have real jobs. I fear them. [Laughing] My father was a professional television writer. I was taken aside by him and told, "Son, whatever you do, please do not write for television. It is really hard work." I was always kind of an anti-TV snob because I wasn't a huge fan of television growing up. However, that changed later on in my life.

AMY SHERMAN-PALLADINO: Growing up, my father was, and still is, a professional comic. My mother was a professional dancer. So, I grew up in a show-business family that had the attitude, "You want to go to college? What's that for?" I did take a lot of dance classes and acting classes. Many of my father's friends were comedians, and since they hung around our house, I was exposed to comedy at an early age. I knew about Lenny Bruce when I was very, very young. I think that atmosphere really helped me with my writing.

BILL LAWRENCE: I am one of those lucky guys who has reached 35 with my parents still together. They have always been unbelievably supportive of me. I wanted to try to be a writer right after high school. I didn't know exactly what kind of writer, but I knew that I wanted to become a writer. The only thing my parents said to me was that they wanted me to go to college first. They said I didn't have to do extremely well, but they just wanted me to graduate. If I did that, they agreed that they'd support me and help me out financially if I got stuck for rent or something like that. They told me that if I skipped college and went the writing route right after high school, I would have their emotional support, but not their financial support. So, it was their way of kind of bribing me to make me go to college. I'm glad that I did. In retrospect, I can tell you that it was great.

The only classes that I really liked in college were my creative writing courses. I spent four years working on my writing. I went to William and Mary. They didn't have television or film departments. It's one of the oldest colleges in America. All the writing professors were gray-haired guys who looked like Mr. Chips. In college, I wrote more dialogue-heavy pieces than the other students.

My parents always encouraged me and told me from an early age that I could do, or be, anything I wanted to. It was very cool. Since I was aware of so many people in Hollywood with dysfunctional family backgrounds, the fact that my parents fully supported me was a huge leg up. My father is a career businessman and, when I was just starting out in L.A., every once in a while I would get a phone call from a friend of his who worked on the East Coast for some large company. I was familiar with the people who would call, but down deep, I knew that they would never call me unless my dad asked them to. They would phone politely and say, "Hey, Bill we have an opening here in marketing at Pepsi and we were just thinking about you for the position." I usually answered with something like, "No thanks. I am fine." But, that's the kind of thoughtful parenting I was fortunate enough to have.

BARBARA HALL: My family did not encourage me toward a life of writing. They did not understand what that was all about. So, writing was a form of rebellion for me. The "encouragement" just came from within me as a result of my sort of contrary nature.

I grew up in a small town in Southern Virginia, where there were a handful of professions you could pursue, and writing wasn't one of them. I remember teachers telling me that it was hard to try to become a writer. I did have a couple of teachers who encouraged me in terms of my interest in literature, but not in my interest in trying to commit to it. Later, when I got to college at James Madison University, I found a creative community where we all encouraged each other. Then, the other source of encouragement to be creative was through my interest and participation in music. I became obsessed with music. First, at a very young age, I learned to play the guitar and then went on to become a member of a band, which I still am. I was also a rock critic for a few years.

JONATHAN STARK: When you're young and want to get into something creative, most parents say, "You really need something that you can fall back on."

My mother pushed me to become a teacher. Growing up, my brother and sister were always funny, and I think that was a good influence on me. My father passed away when I was nine years old, and being funny sometimes develops when you have somewhat of a tragic life. I would compensate for that by being funny and making people laugh. I think it also makes you feel better. I have worked with a lot of writers who have come out of dysfunctional families. Sometimes it is the better base to write from.

MAX MUTCHNICK: I have to thank my mother for turning me on to the world of writing situation-comedy at a young age. My mother worked on the Paramount lot, and I was on the sets of so many great shows. I was a latch-key kid. After school, I had to get into a cab and go to the Paramount lot to see my mom. I watched every television show that Paramount launched in those years of my childhood. I sat in the stands and watched rehearsals of top shows. I watched Jerry Paris direct *Happy Days* and Alan Rafkin direct *Laverne & Shirley*. To see these shows unfold in front me of me was amazing. I remember falling head over heels for this world of television production. I knew it was a world that I had to be a part of.

YVETTE LEE BOWSER: I came from a single-parent home and a lower-middle-class background. I wouldn't say, specifically, that I was motivated creatively by my mother, but she did encourage me to achieve. My mother was more than disappointed that I did not want to go to law school and that I wanted to pursue a career writing jokes. She thought that was the most hilarious thing she'd ever heard. The idea of me wanting to bypass law school and, basically, get paid nothing to be an apprentice in order to discover what television writing was about was a little devastating for her at first. But I was determined to make it work. As destiny would have it, I have been a working writer for the past 17 years.

TOM FONTANA: My brother opened my eyes to a lot of great creative experiences at a young age. While I was going to high school, my brother was going to college in Buffalo. He was in the theater program. I started hanging out with him and the grown-ups. I started acting in the plays, even though I never wanted to be an actor. I played roles like the "third spear-carrier" or "pizza delivery boy." I was actually in two plays that Diane English wrote, because we went to college together. Diane English went on to create the television show *Murphy Brown*.

The Influence of Other Writers

ALAN BALL: Certainly among the writers that I responded to a lot when I was young was Tennessee Williams. I grew up in the South and my family had its own gothic edge. In Williams' works, the language is beautiful and the characters are so compelling while being deeply flawed. Yet, they're not bad people. They just wanted to be loved like everyone else. I was also influenced by those great old warhorses of post-war American drama—William Inge and Arthur Miller. However, I guess Tennessee Williams had the biggest effect on me as a writer since he was the first dramatist I was aware of other than Shakespeare. I really loved the plays *One Flew Over the Cuckoo's Nest* and *Sometimes a Great Notion*. When I started becoming aware of filmmakers and directors and their sensibilities, I immediately responded to Robert Altman and Woody Allen. I am still a fan of Woody Allen, who, even at his worst, is still a lot smarter than most of what we see in mainstream entertainment.

BRENDA HAMPTON: I read a lot during my childhood and I still do. I think my writing influences actually started in high school. I have read many, many books and have been influenced by the writing of everyone from Mark Twain to Tennessee Williams. I was always into different writers at different times in my life. In high school, I really loved the legendary author James Joyce. I liked Joyce because I like impressionist art. His impressionistic writing appealed to me because it had a feeling to it that is complicated and interesting to read.

MARK BRAZILL: I didn't go to college, but I did read a lot of books during my youth. My sister is 10 years older than me. When I was a kid growing up, she would give me books like *Lord of the Flies*. She gave me Kurt Vonnegut to read when I was only nine years old and I really liked his work. I thought Vonnegut was a great writer and had a sense of humor that I could understand. Richard Pryor and his comedic writing had a huge influence on me as well. Also, not so much hearing the comedian Lenny Bruce, but seeing what Lenny Bruce had to say and how he said it had a big effect on me. Woody Allen with his film writing had a huge influence on me, too. *Love and Death* is one of my favorite Woody Allen films, which actually is not one of his most famous films. I also really liked his films *Sleeper* and *Crimes and Misdemeanors,* which is my favorite movie ever made.

BILL LAWRENCE: I thought Larry Gelbart was an unbelievably good writer. He was, of course, the head writer and creator of *M*A*S*H*. I also saw musicals that were written by Gelbart as well. I was a big Neil Simon fan, too. Once I started getting more mature and became savvy toward TV, I really got into the Charles brothers. They wrote and created hit shows like *Taxi* and *Cheers*. I felt that they were really solid dialogue writers, not your ordinary joke writers. When you were young, you remembered *Happy Days,* where the big joke might have been "Exactamundo!" That was funny, but cheesy. Then, as I got older, and watched *Taxi* and *Cheers,* I realized the jokes were much more subtle, sophisticated, and really appealed to my personal sense of humor. I was a huge book nerd and theater geek, masquerading as a jock, when I was growing up. I was a huge Joseph Heller fan and admired his wonderful dialogue in the book *Catch-22.* I remember how surreal, sharp, and funny it was. *Biloxi Blues* was wonderful, too.

DENNIS LEONI: I really loved reading Louis L'Amour novels. I also enjoyed Mark Twain. One of the books that had the most profound effect on me during my youth was J.D. Salinger's *Catcher in the Rye.* I've had that dream of being *The Catcher in the Rye,* the very same way Holden Caulfield had. Other books that I enjoyed were *Great Expectations* by Charles Dickens, *The Red Badge of Courage* by Stephen Crane, and most of those classic stories that we had to read as part of our school curriculum growing up. Then, when I attended the University of Arizona, I took Russian literature and I was introduced to Russian authors, like Leo Tolstoy and Anton Chekov. As I got older, I read more and more Western stories, a favorite being *Lonesome Dove* by Larry McMurtry. He is one of the greatest living American authors, and *Lonesome Dove* is truly one of my favorite books of all time. It won a Pulitzer Prize. I also think Truman Capote was a tremendous writer. Stephen King and Pat Conroy are terrific writers as well. The book *The Milagro Beanfield Wars*, written by John Nichols, had a great effect on me. It really brought me back to my Mexican-American culture because I had grown up and moved away from it. As you can see, throughout my life, I've always had a varied taste in literature.

BARBARA HALL: There were definitely writers who influenced me, but they were all novelists. I wasn't even aware that there were television writers during my youth. I was influenced heavily by the Southern literature written by William Faulkner and Flannery O'Connor. I was also influenced by a lot of poets like Robert Frost and just too many other poets to name. I would sit in my room and read the writing of these wonderful poets and not even really understand it. However, I wanted to read it. The single biggest influence in my young creative life was Bruce Springsteen. He influenced me because his music combined everything that I wanted to do with music. I was fascinated by it because it was sort of poetry, street poetry. It also reflected my kind of people—working-class people. Springsteen was someone who took the life I was living and romanticized it and made it poetic. For a long time, I believed I didn't have anything to write about because I was growing up in this small, backwater town. Springsteen really showed me how to do it and validated my existence. All of his songs are about getting out and triumphing and persevering. At least the early stuff was about that. I really needed to hear that because when you live in a small town in the middle of nowhere, every place else in the world seems so far away and every goal seems so impossible. He broke it down for me.

Initiatives into Writing

JOSH SCHWARTZ: I wanted to become a writer since I was seven years old. It first occurred to me when I was at sleep-away summer camp and they had an essay-writing contest. The winner won an ice cream sundae, and when you are eating camp food, that's the best prize you can hope for. [Laughing] Other kids wrote things like, "Why I like soccer" or "What I did this summer." The first line of my essay was, "Spielberg has done it again!" It was all about his then-new film, *Gremlins*. My essay won the contest! I got the ice cream sundae and I was on my way to becoming a writer. I always kept journals and wrote James Bond-style short stories and sitcom stuff. In fourth and fifth grade, I was writing actual dialogue in those journals.

ILENE CHAIKEN: When I was very young, in my elementary school days, I was the official school poet. I wrote terrible poems and was not a child genius by any means. However, I guess by suburban Philadelphia elementary-school standards, I qualified. I was asked to write poems every time there was a significant event in my elementary school. So, I did get into creative writing for a while. Then I completely lost the thread and gave up writing completely. I had a boyfriend whom I was very influenced by who told me that writing was obsolete. He told me that I had to find a more dynamic medium to work in. I then went on to study art.

LARRY DAVID: I did not do a lot of writing as a child, except to make up book reports for school, so cheating was my first foray into creativity. By the way, the word "creative" was not bandied about in my house. We were raised to make a living, not "express" ourselves. I did not really start writing dialogue until I wrote the screenplay for a feature film in 1978. The screenplay was a comedy about the explorer Ponce de Leon, who went looking for the Fountain of Youth. Could that be possible? Did an explorer actually approach Queen Isabella and King Ferdinand and ask them for ships so he could look for the Fountain of Youth? And they said, "Yes, sure. Go ahead." To me, that's fascinating. I could talk about it for hours. What about the crew? What did Ponce tell them? How could they take orders from this nut?

BARBARA HALL: I first started writing poetry when I was eight years old. When I was in Chatham High School in Virginia, I was the poet laureate. That was mainly because it never occurred to anyone else in my school to write poetry. That became my identity. For instance, I was the person to write the poem for the prom program. I fell in love with poetry and stayed with it for a while, even studying poetry in college. I also wrote short stories with my sister, who also went on to become a television writer. I honestly can't remember a time in my life when I was not writing. In college, I did every form of writing. I even fell in love with journalism for a while. So, my life has always been about writing and I have tried a little bit of everything.

SHAWN RYAN: I won a playwriting contest in college, and one of my plays was entered into the American College Theater Festival. The play that I had written ended up winning "Best Original Play" in the New England region of that competition and it won "Best Comedy" nationwide. Because of the acclaim of my play, I was rewarded by being brought out to L.A. to spend a few weeks hanging out in the writers' room of *My Two Dads,* to see how professional writers operate.

BRENDA HAMPTON: I had a poem published in the church newsletter when I was in third grade. I then worked on the school newspaper in high school. As far as storytelling goes, I think the first form of my own storytelling was when I started writing a novel when I lived in Chattanooga, Tennessee. I also think that was probably my first attempt at creative writing. The book was about a criminal case that started in Chattanooga. What I wanted to do was tell the story about a murder, which was a true story. Since the taped confession was part of the court record, I was able to get a copy of it because it became public domain. So, I wanted to write the novel and then put the tape in the back of the book so you didn't know who killed the woman until you played the tape. However, by the time I was halfway through writing the novel, the guy who reportedly killed her was let out of prison. I never finished that novel, but that was my first attempt at storytelling.

BILL LAWRENCE: I was never that great a student, but I always really enjoyed reading books, seeing plays, and watching movies and TV shows. I wanted to become a writer from a very young age. I always thought it was incredible fun. I even went through the period of high school where I was on the basketball team and I hung out with the jocks, but, at the same time, I also worked on the literary magazine. So, I went through that whole 16-year-old thing where you pretend you do not want to do something. I used the excuse that the reason I wrote for the literary magazine was because it would help me get into college. But, underneath it all, I loved it. I loved writing stories and I loved reading. I'm sure it's similar to the burden that kids go through who like the theater. When you are in high school or junior high and you want to be on the stage in musicals, there is a certain stigma connected with it. I can compare it with being on the literary magazine because you can be perceived as a literary magazine nerd. This was very much the atmosphere, because I was a public-school kid. I loved writing for the school magazine, but part of the game for me was pretending that I didn't even like doing it. At that age you usually don't think about writing TV stuff. I was definitely into writing short stories. Coming out to L.A. and becoming a TV writer didn't really occur to me until after college.

YVETTE LEE BOWSER: I was interested in writing from a very early age. When it was "Show and Tell" in school, I would always bring my puppets and have a little puppet show. As early as elementary school, I would write the little skits for the puppet shows. In fact, the first thing that I had written that resembled dialogue was in my *Raggedy Ann and Andy* puppet show. I remember my first puppet show very clearly. It was about Raggedy Ann and the Fairy Godmother and a tooth that was placed under a pillow. Somehow, no money was left for the missing tooth. Raggedy Ann and Andy had to go on a journey to find the tooth and there was some life lesson contained in it, but I don't remember what it was. [Laughing] I do remember that they did live happily ever after and they did find the tooth. I also wrote a little book about a hen, and my mother still has it in her garage. So, I have always been a writer of sorts.

I was a journalist in high school and college and here I am now writing for a living. It is a wonderful offshoot of all of that. I also kept a diary for a long time. And, now when I am trying to create a show or episodes for a show, I figuratively, not literally, am ripping pages out of my diary and telling my personal story in some form or other. When I originally wrote in it during my youth, there was no intention to use the information in it later. The only intention was to write down my own thoughts at the moment. It is a wonderful experience for me to review those memories. Not too many people can really tell their own personal story, but I have really had the benefit and the advantage of kind of chronicling my own life and utilizing it in my television writing career.

I worked my way up to a writer's position on a show called *A Different World,* which was about young people who were in college, and I was just out of college. There I was telling my own college stories through those characters. I later went on to create a show about young people just out of college who were trying to make sense of their lives. That was called *Living Single.* Then, I created a show called *For Your Love,* which chronicled the many stages of relationships that I went through in my own life. For instance, commitment-phobic relationships, newly wedded bliss, and finally dedicated veterans. I am currently a dedicated veteran. So, I have been extremely lucky in my career to be able to have the opportunity to write about my own experiences in the shows I have worked on and created.

TOM FONTANA: I come from a big Italian family, and one night to shut us up my parents took us to a play, *Alice in Wonderland,* at the Studio Arena Theater in Buffalo. I remember going home that night and writing dialogue. The show motivated me to want to write. I went on to write stupid stories and then advanced to writing plays. I even wrote the senior play in my high school. It was the first thing I ever had produced.

AMY SHERMAN-PALLADINO: The earliest thing that resembled a form of dialogue between characters that I wrote were various plays for my mother's children's theater group. That was really done under duress, because she actually forced me to do it. I originally wanted to be a dancer in the Broadway show *Cats.* I did not have any interest in any profession that put you in an office, which required you to sit in a chair all day. However, that eventually changed when I attended college, where I became interested in writing more and more.

Education

JOSS WHEDON: I went to Wesleyan College, where I studied film and had extraordinarily brilliant professors. I watched as many movies as I possibly could put my paws on. It was all film, all the time. It was great! I loved films like Alfred Hitchcock's *Vertigo* and Vincente Minnelli's *The Bad and the Beautiful*. It was a grand time. I miss it mainly because it was the most concentrated, intense amount of work in my life until I created the television show *Buffy the Vampire Slayer*. In college, I was exposed to every damn thing and my brain was exploding with creative thoughts. In fact, I gave up everything else and just concentrated on film. Later, I sort of realized that all of the other stuff I dabbled in during my youth turned out to be very useful. For instance, the elements of storytelling were key.

ILENE CHAIKEN: I went to art school at the Rhode Island School of Design, where I spent a couple of years trying to become a graphic designer. I never really had the talent to be a graphic designer and really only wanted to tell stories. So in a compromise, I switched into the film department. By doing so, I found a medium that addressed my boyfriend's issues and also allowed me to do the thing I was originally compelled to do. There was a dual film program involving my school and Brown University. They had reciprocal film programs. I took most of my film-theory courses at Brown and learned most of what I know about film from those courses. The film department at Rhode Island School of Design was actually a visual-arts film department. It was not at all about narrative storytelling. There were professors of film there who exhibited their films at the Museum of Modern Art. I started making movies that told stories, and something inspirational happened while I was making my thesis film. I was in the process of editing my film when some visiting critics came by. There were three men standing over my shoulder, looking at what I was doing, and they said to me, "You are going to go to Hollywood."

J.J. ABRAMS: I went to Sarah Lawrence College in New York. We didn't really have majors there. I didn't want to take the nonfiction essay course I was enrolled in, but I couldn't switch out of it. In that class, I started writing fiction as nonfiction. I tried to pass it off as nonfiction, so, in essence, it really turned out to be a great fiction class. That course helped me a lot in my future writing.

DENNIS LEONI: I spent two years at the University of Arizona. I was a public administration major and I was on track to become a bureaucrat. I'm happy that I didn't do that for a career. I left right before my junior year because I got it into my head that I wanted to become an actor. I broke away from school because I was bored and did not see the practical application of these subjects to real life. I am a bit of a pragmatist and said to myself, "Why do I need economics? Why do I need ethics? I'm an ethical person already." Now, I realize it didn't really have anything to do with that. However, I felt school was not the right thing for me.

ALAN BALL: I have always been writing and started at a very early age. I was writing puppet shows as a young child. In high school, I was writing skits for pep rallies. So, I've always felt comfortable as a writer, and I genuinely feel that was what I was born to do. It wasn't until I got into college at Florida State University that I decided to major in theater. Like everybody, I wanted to become an actor. I started writing as a way to create roles for myself, because I wasn't getting cast in anything in college.

JOSH SCHWARTZ: I went to film school at USC. I was in the undergraduate screenwriting program. I actually wound up never graduating, and let me explain why: When I was a sophomore, we had to write our first feature-length script as a class project. I wrote a script entitled *Providence*. It was based on my senior year in high school, and was all about the experience of meeting the love of one's life right when life is about to begin. You know what I'm talking about? You finally meet this person who you actually love, but your lives are going off into opposite directions and you can't be together. That's a very special developmental stage of young life. Everyone said to me, "Don't write a movie script about high school. It's so cliché. Everyone does that for their first script." I felt that this is what I wanted to write and, after all, it was my first script. So, the topic seemed appropriate. I finished it in the spring, which was the end of my sophomore year in college. Right before I left, there was a writing contest called The Nicholson Screenwriting Award, and I dropped off my script in the contest box. I ended up winning! The prize was $12,000, which, in college, is a ton of cash. The only problem was that you had to be a junior or older to enter. So, I had to take it back because I was only a sophomore. Then, a friend of mine in college, who was coincidentally working at a production company, said that he loved the script. It landed in the hands of a manager named Warren Zide. He read it and liked it. Warren had me come in to meet him in the fall of my junior year. The film wound up being sold to Columbia/Sony Pictures for a lot of money. It was a really surreal time for me. Television stations wound up coming to my fraternity house, wanting to talk to me about the sale of the film script. Jules

Asner from E! Entertainment Television came down to the fraternity house to interview me. Then, I had all sorts of other agents calling to represent me and wanting to hang out at college parties. It was a very weird time in my life.

YVETTE LEE BOWSER: I went to Stanford University and I studied political science and psychology. Actually, all of political science is writing. Even when you are telling your personal stories in half-hour or hour-long formats for television, there are subjects like politics, psychology, and sociology involved. Therefore, I find that what I know from obtaining my college degree and from my own experiences and formal learning have played a role in my being a sitcom writer. I enjoy certain reality shows like *Survivor* because of the sociology and politics of it. I look at it in a more analytical way. You can look at college in a more simplistic and universal way, too, because I feel that a college education gives you a broader spectrum from which to think. College experience gives you more resources and different angles from which to analyze life and why things are happening the way they are happening in various situations. At Stanford, the motto was, "Question authority." I have learned that you also have to question authority in television. I tend to question authority when people tell me how characters should act or how a story should unfold. So, the exposure and formal training I had in college has played an important role in the person that I've become. I find different questions to ask and to answer via my storytelling. This keeps it fresh for me and for audiences watching the show.

JONATHAN STARK: I grew up in Erie, Pennsylvania, and went to a small college there called Mercyhurst. I was getting my teaching degree, but used to hang out with the theater people. My best friend and roommate at the time was Michael Patrick King, who has gone on to become a very successful television writer for shows like *Sex and the City*. It wasn't a show-business-oriented school, but Michael and I wound up succeeding in the business.

LARRY DAVID: I went to the University of Maryland, and I didn't really do any writing there. I was kind of a screw-off. I always took the easy way out by studying for tests at the very last minute. I was lazy, as most comedians are. Comedians are lazy people. We don't even like to pee. It's a schlep. It takes time. Who needs it? Most comedians don't even work on their material. If something occurs to them, they'll write it down, which in and of itself is work. "Oh no, I have to take my pen out and write this down. Why did I have to think of this?"

Breaking In

The First Job in TV

BARBARA HALL: My first job in television was writing. However, the very first thing I wrote when I moved to L.A. was a novel. That novel got the attention of a television agent, who wanted to know if I wanted to write for TV. I was young and just wanted to make a living as a writer. So, I didn't care. I pretty much fell into television writing in a weird way and then wound up liking it. Actually, I didn't like it right away, but learned that I had a certain knack for it. I started in comedy and it was not a place I wanted to stay because I didn't like that particular writing process. *Family Ties* was my first freelance script, and the first show I was staffed on was *Newhart*. I didn't like the "room writing process." I was too much of an introvert for that. Then, I found my way to drama and worked on the first show of Joshua Brand and John Falsey, *A Year in the Life*. I then went on to do all of their shows, including *I'll Fly Away* and *Northern Exposure*. You can say that through them, I really found a home writing drama.

LARRY DAVID: My first job in television was performing on a TV show called *Fridays*, which was ABC's ersatz *SNL*. The producers of the show were going around to comedy clubs to cast, and I was doing stand-up in New York City's Catch a Rising Star when, lo and behold, I got the job. Something good happened to me. It was inconceivable, because at the time I was preparing for life as a homeless person. When I walked around New York, I would take note of good places where I might have to sleep one day. Anyway, the show lasted for two years. There were some things about it that I had problems with, but I did get to write and perform in my own sketches for the first time, and I made great, lifelong friends. I didn't care for the fact that the show was live. I'm not good with live in life, much less on TV. In fact, that's the problem with life. It's live.

MARK BRAZILL: My first real job in TV was as a writer. I was a comic until 1990 and I appeared on some television shows, but nothing ever that spectacular. Then, I opened for Dennis Miller at the Improv in Cleveland. He liked my work and asked me, "If I get a TV show, would you write for it?" I said, "Sure, that would be great." Miller got a TV show in 1991, which was the first *Dennis Miller Show*. It was shot in L.A. and it aired on The Chicago Tribune Network. Then, my wife got pregnant with my son and I did not want to go on the road anymore. I then became a full-time television writer, and I wrote for several shows while also creating a lot of pilots. I also wrote for *In Living Color*. Then, when I met writers Bonnie and Terry Turner, I got hired on their show *3rd Rock from the Sun*. That's when my professional life really started taking shape.

DAVE HACKEL: After I was done with college, I worked at a local television station in Columbus, Ohio. While I was there, we did four hours of original and local programming every day. Since we had no budget, we had to get pretty inventive. For instance, we interviewed firemen and policemen, did talk shows, and even produced cooking shows. From working there, I learned a great deal about the technical side of television. What I liked the most about it was the wonderful feeling I had of accomplishment, because we would start a project with just an idea and end up with an entire television show. It was a real high for me. When that job ended, I moved out to Los Angeles. I figured if I was going to work in this business and be unemployed, I might as well be warm, right?

TRACY NEWMAN: My first job in television was in New York, where I acted in commercials. Before I became a writer, I did various things as a performer. Actually, Ed McMahon acted as my manager. Ed and I went to the same vocal coach, he saw me perform, and took me on as a client. He put me on *The Tonight Show* in 1965, where I sang a Bob Dylan song and another one. I was mediocre at best. In 1974, I was on *The Tonight Show* again, doing card tricks. So, I had various careers in TV before I settled into writing.

DAVID KOHAN: My father and Garry Marshall, who created hit shows like *Happy Days* and *Laverne & Shirley,* used to work together in New York. They first met when they were in the Army together. So, when I first came to Los Angeles and I wanted a job in the entertainment business, I went to "Camp Garry Marshall." [Laughing] Garry had four shows going at one time on the Paramount lot, and he was a happy camp director. I looked around and saw all these people writing, acting, and directing. I thought, "I could do this for a living at some point in my life." That idea of television being accessible and open to me stayed in my mind and close to my heart for many years to come. Most people who go to school on the East Coast have parents who are businessmen, doctors, or lawyers. They look at the entertainment business and think it is a hermetically sealed world with no point of entry. I thought the complete opposite way. I used to think to myself, "Working in TV is what I could do for a living, but how the hell do you become a doctor?"

YVETTE LEE BOWSER: I knew someone who knew Bill Cosby. I called that person and begged him to introduce me to Mr. Cosby, so that I could beg him for a job. [Laughing] I was willing to get coffee and sandwiches or whatever else I needed to do to get experience to understand what television was all about.

I knew that I wanted to write, but I didn't really know what that entailed on a sitcom. Anyway, I got the wonderful opportunity to meet Mr. Cosby during my senior year of college. What happened was that Mr. Cosby was shooting a movie in Oakland, California, not far from Stanford. So, I went up to the film set and met him. I showed him a few of my short stories and he chuckled a bit. Then, Mr. Cosby advised me, "Go to law school. There ain't nothing for you out here!" I think he said that to me to see how tough I really was and how much I genuinely wanted this as a career. I see it as Mr. Cosby wanting me to get used to hearing "No," because he knew that I was going to hear a lot of rejection in this business. Mr. Cosby was kind enough to introduce me to a very nice couple who said they were willing to pay for me to go to law school. Cosby did that because he knew I was faced with the expense of law school and I had already incurred a big debt at Stanford, even though I had received some scholarships and grants. There was also something in my gut, eating at me, saying, "There is definitely something else for you." I then said to Mr. Cosby, "Please, I really feel that working in television is what I should be doing, even though I don't know exactly what it entails." I explained that I possessed this creative energy that I felt had to be tapped and I would love to have the opportunity to be exposed to TV writers. Also, I said that I hoped to find out first-hand if it is or if it isn't for me. Mr. Cosby essentially gave me my first opportunity to fail when he hired me as an apprentice on *A Different World*, and I made the best out of it.

ILENE CHAIKEN: My first job in TV was working for Aaron Spelling. Before that, I had been working on movies. I had been an agent trainee and then a development executive. I wound up at Spelling's company with a movie producer because I had been his development person. I then met Aaron Spelling, and I think he liked me, because he offered me a job in the TV side of his company. I started there and wound up, over a five-year period, going from being the TV development person to running the whole department. I learned everything about television and how it works. I learned a lot from watching Aaron Spelling work. I honestly didn't really love being an executive. I wasn't born to do it and it doesn't suit me all that well. But, I am fairly driven, so I got pretty successful at it. At the same time, I was also pretty miserable.

My very last job as an executive was running Quincy Jones Entertainment. I went over there as the senior creative executive under a corporate executive who got fired. I wound up doing the whole job: I was running the film and television departments. It was a brand-new company, a joint venture with Warner Brothers. We were getting the whole thing off the ground and put one television show on the air, which was *The Fresh Prince of Bel-Air*. I was intricately involved as an executive in putting that show together. I was really immersed in the job and having a great time, largely because Quincy Jones is a fascinating person to work for. He is wildly creative, intriguing, and connected. Unfortunately, the job also became very political. There were a lot of the people in the company, and each one wanted a lot of things. I just crashed and burned in that job with enormous intensity.

DENNIS LEONI: I started in the entertainment business as an actor and a stuntman on a Western movie location in Old Tucson. It was really my fantasy ever since I was a young boy to be a cowboy, and I got the opportunity to live that life for a while at Old Tucson. They shot hundreds of Westerns there, including John Wayne movies. We also used to do Wild West shows for all of the people who came to visit. I would fall off a building five days a week, and I did that for a couple of years. When the movies came into town to film, we would get bit parts.

My very first appearance on film was for an Encyclopedia Britannica production, where I played a Mexican farmer. I then appeared in an actual movie called *Another Man, Another Chance*, starring James Caan. Of course, you can't see me because I spend most of my time on camera in the dust of James Caan's horse as I ride behind him. [Laughing]

Then, I decided to go to Hawaii because people told me that I look Hawaiian. I got the idea that I could work on *Hawaii Five-O*. My about-to-be wife and I moved to Hawaii. I walked into the offices of *Hawaii Five-O*, and I projected an attitude like "Here I am! God's gift." [Laughing] To my surprise, even though they did not hire me as an actor, they did hire me as an extra. I didn't have any money and it all seemed the same to me at the time, except that actors got paid more. Eventually, they found out that I had stunt experience. So, they let me double Jack Lord because I was his size. Initially, they put me in a blue suit and a wig and up I went in a helicopter because Jack didn't want to fly in one. He apparently thought it was going to crash or something. Eventually, they hired me as a stand-in and this was good because it was steady employment. They would pay me $500 to crash a car or race a car, which I ironically had no experience doing, but successfully did. I came from Tucson and was more accustomed to stunts on horses. But, when you are young and ambitious, you think you can do anything.

I ultimately worked my way from in front of the camera to behind the camera. One day, assistant director Don-Martin Nielsen handed me a radio and said, "I need help. You are now a production assistant." I became a PA. Then, one day Don-Martin called in sick and I became an assistant director. He taught me everything about the business. When I received the Lemme Award from the National Latino Entertainment Organization, Don-Martin came and spoke on my behalf.

What got me into writing was when I started reading *Hawaii Five-O* scripts and I thought to myself, "These are not that great. I could do better." I then wrote a two-hour pilot called *Alexandro*, which was a Western. *Alexandro* is not spelled with a "j" but with an "x," because the story is about a Mexican kid who becomes Anglified. Then, I got married and we moved to L.A. I had this two-hour script in my hand, $3,000 in my pocket, and an old Ford pickup truck. I got an agent. However, I never sold that particular script, but I think that people in the business thought I had potential.

Deciding on a Writing Partner

MAX MUTCHNICK: There is a picture next to you on that table of my writing partner, David [Kohan], and I from high school. We were 15 and 16 years old, performing in a production of *West Side Story* at Beverly Hills High School. David played the part of Riff and I played Baby John. That was where David and I first met. When we both started out, we thought that we would be solo career guys with spotlights on us and we would rise to wherever we wanted to go in life. It hasn't been like that at all. We have been a team since "day one" and have stuck by each other. I don't think either of us would have had it any other way. Having this close partnership is a comfort zone for us in terms of our careers. It is a wonderful touchstone that we sit across from each other and that we have looked in each other's faces since we were 15 and 16. Whose ego can really get carried away in a situation like this? The relationship has taken on a much more familiar vibe than anything else in our business lives because that is how we are most comfortable. Between the two of us, there is one very big life here with a bunch of different styles and tastes. So, it makes the base from where we are creating a lot stronger. This partnership is working right now, and we have no plans to switch to something different. The dynamic is a reality for both of us and it's building solidly to becoming a happy and healthy future.

DAVID KOHAN: Having a writing partner is great for a number of reasons. It is great to have someone to share triumphs with and it is great having someone to help dissipate setbacks with. It is easier to absorb the hits and knocks when you have someone going through the negatives with you. Also, I'd like to mention the fact that Max [Mutchnick] has a brother who is less than two years older than he is and I have a twin brother. We have great relationships with our respective brothers. So, working together is something that we understand through life experience. We knew from an early age how to work with a guy who is close to your age whom you negotiate things with effectively and get along with. There are similarities in my relationship with Max that we have had with our own brothers. For instance, we have complimentary strengths. We have similar goals and a mutual respect for one another. Aren't all those the qualities that make for a good marriage?

TRACY NEWMAN: I think if you can write alone, then do it alone. But, if you feel you absolutely can't write alone, then having a writing partner is a great way to do it and it is often more fun. Having a partner to kick ideas around with can make the writing process a lot easier. Also, one very positive thing about our particular relationship is that we never goof off much.

When Jonathan [Stark] and I started writing together, we were just sort of friends, but we didn't hang out too much outside of writing. When we would meet up to write, we would maybe talk for 10 minutes about what was going on in our lives, but then we would get right down to work. We would then work very, very intensely for four or five hours straight, which was our limit. We really worked during those five hours, and I think that is the key to a successful relationship. It's about the need for a partner and about the fun of having one, but underneath it all, it's really about concentrating on the work and keeping each other right on target.

Over the years, as writing partners, we have had a lot of fights, but we have also had a lot of laughter, and that is what counts. I always know that John is going to make me laugh, and every once in a while I make him laugh. Basically, that is what makes it all worthwhile as partners. You do take the pressure off each other when it's needed.

JONATHAN STARK: During the first spec script we wrote, I was depressed about an old girlfriend. I called my writing partner on the phone and said, "Tracy, I am too depressed to write. Can you write the script?" She replied, "You really want me to write it alone?" Well, she wound up writing most of it herself. I eventually came over and we started working on it. However, she supported me when I needed it the most, and that is a very important part of having a compatible writing partner. I think you have to make sure that you find a writing partner who you can have a really close sense of humor with. If the relationship is off base and you don't tune in to each other, then writing together is not going to be that much fun.

Writing Spec Scripts

JOSS WHEDON: The first spec script I wrote was for a TV show called *Just in Time*. The show got cancelled before I finished the script. My friend who was the executive producer asked me if I had anything else that he could read. I said, "No, but if you tell me about your show, I could write a spec for it." Then, I wrote a few more scripts, including a *Roseanne* spec. That spec was what got me hired as a staff writer on *Roseanne*. Watching the first season of *Roseanne*, I was completely blown away. I had never seen a sitcom that was written that well. I knew that the spec script I was writing was not as good as the show I was watching, which was very daunting.

DAVID KOHAN: I was Sydney Pollack's assistant, and I did a terrible a job working for him. I was a really, really bad assistant. Finally, after two years of inertia pulling me through a job, I decided that I had to take a leap of faith. I decided to go to New York City to write and try to pull my inspiration from the streets. So, off I went to New York, and after three months of attempting to write, I almost had the colon done after the opening words "FADE IN." [Laughing] Out of the blue, I got a phone call from Max [Mutchnick]. He said, "We started writing together in L.A. and I really feel we never saw it through to fruition." In the middle of his sentence, I interrupted him by saying, "You don't have to say any more. Can you come to New York City and work with me?" Well, Max weighed the pros and cons about coming, and the cons outweighed the pros. But, Max came anyway. Sometimes you have to do that in life. We got a dog named Gus, who was our muse, and over that month, we wrote two spec scripts. One was for *Murphy Brown* and the other was for *Seinfeld*. Max and I were very disciplined. We wrote over that month like it was a job. We took it very seriously.

BRENDA HAMPTON: I wrote a *Roseanne* spec script, and that was in kind of familiar territory. I had actually written for Roseanne Barr earlier when she was doing the comedy club circuit. I also wrote a spec script for *Murphy Brown*. I think the most important thing in writing a spec script if you want to get hired as a staff writer on a sitcom is joke-writing. The reason for that is because you are probably not going to come in and do a first-draft script for a show. You are probably going to get hired as somebody who is going to sit in the room and do joke-writing. So, I feel that is the first place to start. Of course, you have to tell a good story so that the jokes make sense. I think if someone is reading a first-time writer's spec script and they are looking to hire them for a sitcom staff job, first they want to know if they are funny.

BILL LAWRENCE: When I first got out to L.A., I didn't know anything about the process of getting staffed or what kinds of spec scripts to write. In fact, most people don't. What you are really supposed to do is write an episode of one of your favorite shows, and it becomes a virtual résumé for you. So, I was writing a bunch of pilots at first. Unfortunately, that was stupid because I was young and didn't know how to write them. Once I realized that Shapiro and West, the managers I wanted to represent me, executive-produced *Seinfeld,* I went down to the Writers Guild and got a couple of the scripts to see exactly how to format it. I then wrote a bunch of *Seinfeld* scripts and *Wonder Years* scripts. I chose those because I liked both shows and I wanted to become a comedy writer. I also felt that they were not only great shows, but also very different shows. *Seinfeld* was an edgy, joke-driven show and *Wonder Years* had more of a sentimental streak, even though it was a half-hour comedy.

TRACY NEWMAN: Jonathan [Stark] and I wrote a *Cheers* spec script that did not work out. Then we wrote a *Murphy Brown* spec script and we connected with an agent who said the dialogue was good, but we needed to write a fresher story. Then we wrote another *Murphy Brown* spec and that was the one that got us the job as writers on *Cheers.* I essentially learned that when it comes to writing a good spec script, there are three important elements: First, you have to capture the show's characters. Second, it has to be funny. Third, it has to have a good story structure. Once in a great while, I read a spec script where the jokes are so funny that, even though the story structure isn't there, I keep reading. But, 99% of the time, if the story is not pulling me through, I have to stop reading the script and put it down.

AMY SHERMAN-PALLADINO: My then writing partner and I wrote two spec scripts. One was for a show called *Anything But Love,* which I only wrote because I wanted to meet Richard Lewis, whom I had a huge crush on. The other spec script was for *Roseanne.* It was really a timing thing, but within six months of writing those specs we had an agent and we became paid writers on *Roseanne.* They needed chicks and they needed them cheap—and that was us!

DAVE HACKEL: After I was an established writer, I still wrote spec scripts and pretty much reinvented my writing career. Not many professional writers do that. I have actually been on the Paramount lot, with the exception of one year, since 1985. As a writer, I began to get a reputation for working on nice family shows. To be honest, I wasn't enjoying that. I looked up the street of the Paramount lot and saw they were writing and producing shows like *Taxi* and *Cheers*. That was where I wanted to be. Those shows had edgy, sophisticated humor, and I really wanted to be a part of that brand of comedy. I called my agent and said, "I'm going to re-invent myself. I'm going to write all-new material, so don't send out any of my old scripts." After I wrote all-new spec scripts, I ended up writing for the first season of *Dear John*. Then, I got hired to write for *Wings* and stayed there for 129 episodes. After that, I tried to do my own show called *The Pursuit of Happiness,* which didn't really work. Then, I worked on *Frasier* for two and a half years as a consultant. In 1998, I created *Becker* and I have been on *Becker* ever since. Writing those spec scripts took me on a new path and changed my career.

Getting an Agent

ILENE CHAIKEN: I got an agent soon after I decided that I wanted to write. It was at Christmastime in 1991 and I went away to Telluride, Colorado, with my partner and a bunch of friends. I knew that I was going to get fired from my executive job when I got back to L.A. I was really, really angry. I locked myself in that house in Telluride while all my friends went skiing and I wrote a film script. I wrote it in one week. It was called *Esme's Posse*. When I got back to L.A., I sat at my desk for three days until I got the call that I was fired. I then took my script to an agent whom I had worked with and said, "Do something because I can't go back to work as an executive." She agreed to be my agent and got me a job within three weeks writing a movie for Hollywood Pictures. *Esme's Posse* never sold, but it was optioned once or twice. It never even came close to getting made, but it was instrumental in getting me that first job. *Esme's Posse* was a futuristic girl action movie back before it was run of the mill to do female action movies. Based on that script, I got the job writing the first movie I wrote that got made, *Barbed Wire*. The fact that I had been an executive, no matter how unpleasant that experience may have been, was entirely responsible for my navigating my way to a sustained writing career for a couple of years.

BILL LAWRENCE: I lucked out in getting an agent. My mom is an auctioneer in Fairfield County, Connecticut. One of her older clients was Norman Barish, who used to be a writer for *The Dick Van Dyke Show*. After I graduated from college, she hooked me up with Norman. He took a look at my stuff and told me that I write good dialogue and I should try writing some TV scripts. It had never really occurred to me to do that. However, in retrospect I don't know why it never occurred to me because I've always loved television. I actually have an encyclopedia of knowledge in my mind of all the TV shows from my generation. On the other hand, the idea of writing for television had never really occurred to me. Barish advised me to go out to L.A. and give it a shot. He was a huge influence on me. I went out to L.A. with no connections and I was waiting tables and stuff. I called Barish back up and said, "The only people who have read my scripts are my mom, aunt, and friends." He suggested that I show them to an agent. Norman's old agents were George Shapiro and Howard West, but he didn't even know if they were still agents. I was watching *Seinfeld* on my TV one day and I saw that Shapiro and West were listed as executive producers on the show. They were managers, too. I used the Norman Barish connection as an "in" and I harassed those guys for six months. Eventually, I got Howard West to sign me as a client. It was a nice thing to do, because at that stage of their careers, they were not looking to sign on any more clients. They were financially well off, but they signed me anyway and that was my big break.

AMY SHERMAN-PALLADINO: I really believe that getting an agent to represent you all comes down to timing. When my then writing partner and I first entered this business, Hollywood needed women writers, and we had the right material. There are times when being a woman in this business is horrifying. There are other times when it works for you. At that moment, there were not many woman writers in Hollywood. When they are actually looking, there is a smaller playing field for women to play on. That's a reality. At that time, I was 23 and broke. I needed a writing job. It all started because my writing partner Jennifer, who I originally met in college, was teaching traffic school. A writer/ executive broke the law and ended up in the same traffic school. Now, traffic school to Jennifer was only a way to promote our careers. [Laughing] It worked and she basically harassed this man within an inch of his life to read our material. He read it and he liked it. Then, he made some calls to agents and said, "I read these two girls' spec scripts and I think they're great. Please don't bury the scripts. Actually, take a look at them." We then met with a few agencies and decided to sign with William Morris.

MARK BRAZILL: I moved to La Jolla, near San Diego, in 1980 and I started hanging around the Comedy Store in Los Angeles to become a writer for a stand-up comic. You can't really make a living doing that unless you're connected. So, I thought that if I wrote my own stuff and performed it on stage, then maybe I could sell it. I actually sold a piece or two here and there and that was how I started selling my writing.

I was at The Improv in L.A. and a manager who worked at Brillstein-Grey was there. He saw my act, liked my stuff, and then signed me right away. I was lucky to start out at an agency that big. Bernie Brillstein is a dream agent for comics. He represented James Belushi, Dan Aykroyd, Mike Myers, and so many more. He is the best agent for a comic because it usually leads to a job on *Saturday Night Live*. I showcased for *SNL* twice for Lorne Michaels. The first time I showcased, I was in the same showcase as Rob Schneider and David Spade. Of course, they got the jobs because they were tremendous. The second showcase I was in, I was with Chris Rock and Adam Sandler. But, I was never quite as good as I should have been in order to get hired as a performer on *Saturday Night Live*. I was actually very lucky to not get hired for the show because it put me on the road toward becoming a writer. After I gave up the thought of being a performer, I wound up signing with Lanny Noveck at William Morris, and I have been with that agent for 10 years.

DENNIS LEONI: I moved to L.A. and the first thing I did was go to The Writers Guild. They provided a big, long list of agents who will and who will not accept unsolicited material. The new agencies will look at you, but the older, established agencies will only read your material on a recommendation. You have to call the agents and write query letters. You have to start at the bottom and pray that some agent will read your script and like it. That is exactly what happened to me. An agent at the Francine Witkin Agency liked my two-hour pilot, *Alexandro*. He tried to sell it and, of course, nothing ever happened. Then, eventually, my wife, Debbie, got a job at Columbia Television. She worked in the story department. She met a producer named Ike Jones. We became friends and he hired me to write a treatment about The White House. I wrote it and he paid me $4,000. I thought I was rich. The idea that somebody paid me money to write—I thought it was unbelievable! To this day, Ike and I are great friends. He believed in me and gave me my break and I will love him forever. Then Ike introduced me to Jerry Arkoff, who wanted to do a mob movie about the Purple Gang from Detroit. He hired me for $13,000 to write a feature film. Now, I really thought I was rich! [Laughing]

TOM FONTANA: I was a playwright and, not only that, I was a playwright that nobody wanted to produce. I was not a hot ticket in New York theater circles. When I got out to Los Angeles, I didn't have an agent. However, when you go to Los Angeles and you're already working and writing on a show, as I was, it is just like blood being smelled by the hounds. Every agent was all over me to offer representation. I had the attitude that "I already have a job." It was funny being a poor New Yorker and then going to L.A. and suddenly making some real money.

In L.A., there are a few things you need to have to fit into the scene, and one of those things was an agent. So, one of the other writer/producers on *St. Elsewhere*, John Masius, said, "Why don't you use my agent? He's Paul Schwartzman at ICM and he's great." Actually, Paul took me out to an Italian restaurant in Los Angeles. He had lived in Italy prior to that, so we went into the kitchen and he began speaking Italian to the chefs. I thought, "Well that is really cool. If he can go into the kitchen and talk shop with the cooks in Italian, then I want this guy to be my agent." [Laughing] How completely irrelevant can you get? However, that was the deciding factor to me. There was no thought originally in getting an agent at all on my part and that's how it happened.

J.J. ABRAMS: When I was in college, I wrote nine or ten screenplays. I think each one was worse than the one before it. I was just trying to write a screenplay that I liked and I couldn't do it. I was in my senior year of college and while I was on a trip back to L.A., I ran into a friend of mine named Jill Mazursky, who is Paul Mazursky's daughter. When we spoke, she told me to show her some things I had written, and we decided to collaborate on a project together. We wrote a treatment for a film and her father showed it to Jeffrey Katzenberg, who at the time was the head of Disney.

I was back at college, finishing up my senior year and trying to figure out exactly how do you get an agent when Jill called me and told me that her dad showed Jeffrey the treatment and he wanted to buy it. She said, "Let's write the screenplay!" This was something I almost couldn't believe. We sold the treatment and I signed the contracts on a Friday. On that Monday, The Writers Guild strike of 1988 started and lasted for six months. I went back to school and finished my senior year in college.

I went to Los Angeles after graduation and moved into an apartment with my best friend. When the writers' strike was over, we wrote a screenplay for a film that was eventually made: *Taking Care of Business,* starring James Belushi and Charles Grodin. This led to me getting an agent. I met with David Loner, who was at ICM, where Jill was represented. We hit it off, and once the script was sold, he became my agent.

Being Staffed as a Writer

YVETTE LEE BOWSER: I started out as a "scrub" on the show *A Different World*. The theory was that if you trained to write with the writers of the show and you made contributions to the scripts, you would move up the ranks to become an actual writer. So, that was my goal from the first day. I came in pitching ideas for characters and stories. I was tearing pages out of my own diary to come up with storylines. I managed to pitch several characters who became central to the series. I pitched several story ideas that became actual stories for the show that first season. The second season, I was given a staff writing position. My work effort paid off. I became the person that the producers would go to when it was Wednesday and they needed a script by Monday. I wrote about 20 episodes of *A Different World* over the four years I was on the writing staff.

DAVID KOHAN: After Max and I wrote the two spec scripts in New York, we went back to Los Angeles. Our return to L.A. coincided with a need for writers on *The Dennis Miller Show,* which was then a nightly syndicated talk show. They were in need of a couple of writer/producers to come in to do set pieces—jokes, sketches, and cold opens—and we just happened to have material. It wasn't our spec scripts we had just written that got us the job. It was the sketches we had written before. We happened to get these sketches to a showrunner, Dave Thomas, who had just been hired. Dave happened to read them first and said, "Okay." Things seemed to be falling into place for Max and me. At that point, we were confident and felt good about the spec scripts that we had just written. It's really interesting in a way that there is a certain kind of momentum that almost breeds its own luck. You almost put all your energy you have out there in the world and you just feel that, at a certain time, something positive is going to happen, which it did.

MARK BRAZILL: Getting staffed on *3rd Rock from the Sun* was kind of a miracle. I was at a friend's birthday party and it just so happened that writers Bonnie and Terry Turner were there. The Turners are huge in this business. They had written for *Saturday Night Live* for many years. They have also written hit movies like *Tommy Boy, Wayne's World, The Brady Bunch Movie,* and many more. I didn't know the Turners prior to this night, but I certainly knew of them. While I was at the party, I was playing with a nun puppet that somebody gave to my friend as a birthday present. The Turners saw me with the puppet and thought

I was really funny. They said that they were going to produce a new show and asked if I would be interested in writing for it. I didn't have a job, so I immediately said, "Yes." Plus, I felt that it would be an honor to work for them. They sent me the pilot of *3rd Rock from the Sun*. They had already shot a version of it starring John Lithgow. I watched it and felt it was really funny. Who doesn't love John Lithgow? He is such a great actor and one of the nicest guys I've ever met in this business. Years later, when I did the pilot for *That '70s Show*, John left the set of *3rd Rock from the Sun* to go watch the table-read of my show. I was sitting in a wooden industrial chair and John lightly kicked me in the butt. I turned around and he said, "This is so good!" I felt proud and thrilled that he liked the show. I stayed on *3rd Rock from the Sun* for several years. I left for one year to do my own show on NBC called *Mr. Rhodes*, which only lasted one season. I then went back to write for *3rd Rock from the Sun*.

BILL LAWRENCE: I was really lucky. When Howard West signed me, I went from not knowing anybody in L.A. to getting hired on a sitcom staff in just three weeks. The show was called *Billy*, and it was a spin-off of *Head of the Class*. What happens is that you get staffed on a show, and you think it is going to last for three or four years and everything is going to be great. *Billy* only lasted 13 episodes and was cancelled. I was out of work and back to "square one." I was lucky again because I got along with the people I worked with and continued to network with them.

Over the next couple of years, I was able to eek out writing gigs on shows like *Boy Meets World* and *The Nanny*. The tough thing for me is that sometimes in Hollywood (and not just in TV, but in movies, too) it's very easy to get typecast as a certain type of writer. It's similar to the situation where an actor gets typecast. My career had started off as a writer of traditional family comedy, and the only gigs I was getting were those same family comedies. They were not up my alley, but I kept pounding away, even though I didn't enjoy it. I always had this basic philosophy, especially in television, that you always do what you have to do, not necessarily what you want to do. That means you write on shows you do not love and work with people whom you might not respect that much, but always end up working hard and being respectful to them. You must face reality and do whatever you have to so that one day you can take your own shot at something you really want to do.

After a long stretch doing this, I started to reach a point where I felt I'd rather be back East, writing ad copy or doing something else like that. I told my managers that I really didn't want to write family comedies anymore. They were pretty cool about it, fully understood it, and bought into it. Instead of just letting me bail out, they actually produced an edgy play that I wrote. They presented it in Hollywood. From that play, I got signed with a hot TV agency, Broder-Kurland. Ted Chervin has been my agent ever since and has been amazing. From that play, I tried to re-establish myself as something other than a family-show writer. I got the chance to write on the first year of *Friends* that next TV season.

I can never confirm this, but I think that when Ted Chervin signed me, he erased the two years prior to my being repped by him as well as the shows I had worked on. He pitched me to showrunners as a New York playwright and didn't tell anyone about the family comedies I previously wrote on.

I worked on *Friends* for one TV season. *Friends* happened to hit it big. All of a sudden, people who would never interview me before *Friends* were glad to let me come to meet with them on potential new projects. I got lucky because I hooked up with Gary David Goldberg, who originally created *Family Ties,* and we worked together on his briefly aired show *Champs*. We got along very well. *Champs* didn't hit, but as a result of our working relationship, when Michael J. Fox wanted to get back into TV, Gary called me and said, "Let's try to come up with something for Michael." We then created *Spin City*. I was extremely lucky and my advancement at that time was based mostly on the benevolence of others.

LARRY DAVID: My next job after the TV show *Fridays* was writing on *Saturday Night Live*. I got staffed as a writer because I knew a couple of people on the cast and they recommended me. *Saturday Night Live* was somewhat frustrating, because almost all of my sketches were cut, but the work itself was much easier than what I did on *Seinfeld*. It's a lot easier writing a sketch than a half-hour show. One night I got fed up, walked up to the producer before air, and quit. Then, I went back on Monday morning and I pretended it never happened. I later used that as the basis of an episode of *Seinfeld* where George Costanza quits his job. However, in my experience, as opposed to George's, nobody called attention to it at the Monday morning meeting. I stayed on at *Saturday Night Live* for the rest of the '84-'85 season. The best thing about working on *SNL* was that I met Julia Louis-Dreyfus.

BRENDA HAMPTON: The first writing job I was hired on was for a show called *Sister Kate*. The staffing process for me to get hired was very quick. I came out to L.A. to write a book about cancer for Bantam Books. While I was writing that book, a friend of mine from New York, Bill Kenney, called me and asked if I would like to write with him. We wrote a spec script, got an agent, and then got hired as writers on a television show. This all happened in only 30 days.

My book agent introduced me to another agent, who repped TV writers. It's really hard these days to get an agent to represent you. I was very lucky because my book agent knew a TV agent. Since I have had writing assignments since then, I've had no problem getting an agent. I know that many writers who are trying to get into the business find that it is one of the most difficult things to do.

Anyway, after we got hired on *Sister Kate,* there were only three executive producers and us on the writing staff. I worked for three of the nicest, funniest guys in the whole world. We had such a great time and it was a wonderful way to come into the business as a TV writer. I think that the three of them could have written the season by themselves, but they were nice in giving two young people a break. Actually, simply giving two people a break, because I wasn't that young. [Laughing] I think the one thing I did learn from them is that you can write a television series with a very small staff of talented writers.

DAVE HACKEL: The first show I was staffed on was called *Shirley,* starring actress/singer Shirley Jones. It was what is known as an hour-long "dramedy." It was the first time in my career that I was paid to be a writer on a daily basis. Then, we wrote a movie-of-the-week. Around this time, my writing partner and I split up. The first show I was staffed on by myself was *9 to 5,* which was derived from the hit movie *9 to 5,* which starred Dolly Parton. I met another person who became my writing partner on that show, April Kelly. We worked together for a number of years and produced and wrote a show together called *Webster,* starring Emanuel Lewis. We then wrote a feature film script together. In the end, April decided she wanted to study medicine. So, I kept writing comedy on my own.

TOM FONTANA: I went to work in the summer theater in Williamstown, Massachusetts. Blythe Danner was in the company there, and her husband, Bruce Paltrow [the father of Gwyneth Paltrow], was coming to visit. At the time, he had just finished producing *The White Shadow,* which was my father's favorite TV show. I got to know Bruce and he said to me, "I'm doing a medical show and maybe you'd like to come out to Los Angeles to write an episode." I went out to L.A. in the fall of 1981 and wrote the third episode of *St. Elsewhere.* The funny part of that experience was that, up to that point, I had earned a total of $5,000 a year working in theater. So, I asked Bruce, "What do you get to write an hour of TV?" I think, at that time, he told me it was about $15,000 an episode. I said to myself, "I could live for three years on this kind of money! This is like early retirement!" [Laughing] After I wrote the episode, I got hired as a staff writer, eventually becoming a producer and so on.

JONATHAN STARK: Our first writing gig was a morning kids' show called *Wake, Rattle & Roll.* Tracy [Newman] and I split a $500 fee because we were not in the union at the time. Then, we did a show called *They Came from Outer Space.* It was a cross between *Route 66* and *Aliens.* The concept was that aliens came down to Earth, to the United States, bought a Corvette, and drove cross-country, getting into a lot of misadventures. I remember the rewrite note on one of our scripts was, "More women in bikinis." [Laughing] We really wanted to work on another show.

We knew Cherie and Bill Steinkellner, who were executive producers during the tenth season of *Cheers*. Tracy and I knew them from The Groundlings Comedy Club, where Tracy was their teacher for song improvisation. The Steinkellners were performers before they got jobs writing on *Cheers*. Also, I was in a little separate improv company, which Bill directed. Out of the blue, Bill Steinkellner asked me one day, "Why don't you write a TV script?" I think when you do improv, one would assume you can also write. If you can create a scene quickly in your head, you can surely put it down on paper. I was acting at the time and making a living, but I wasn't doing great. So, I began to consider writing for television. I had acted in *Fright Night* and *Project X*. What really got me into writing was the reality that the acting roles started drying up, which often happens in this town. I found myself going on auditions for one-line parts when I had already done lead roles. I then said to myself, "If I'm going to start from the bottom up again, I'd rather start doing something else." So, I asked Tracy to write some spec scripts with me.

JOSS WHEDON: When I got hired as a staff writer on *Roseanne* for the second year, chaos on the show had already descended. Danny Jacobson, who was a writer and producer for *Roseanne* and eventually went on to create *Mad About You*, is really brilliant at finding the emotional truth of a moment and what's funny about it. That's the real basis of all writing. There are things you can learn as a writer working under other people. However, to be honest, I learned more by doing *Buffy* than I learned at *Roseanne*. There still was a lot for me to learn at *Roseanne* because I never studied television writing in school. There is a quality that I have seen in some writers that is just naturally there. What I'm referring to is the ability to find the important moment. I don't think I learned how to write by watching Danny Jacobson, who definitely had that ability. Every good writer or showrunner that I know has that talent. It's simply something you cannot learn. You can learn about structure, payoff, metaphor, and a whole bunch of different things, but not that. I look back at my career before creating *Buffy* and I say to myself, "I was a writer?" But, at the same time, the most important part of writing is empathy. You may not have it in real life. I'm not a particularly observant or even considerate person, except that I can express those qualities in my literary characters. It's something you absolutely must have as a writer, and it's not something I know how to teach.

SHAWN RYAN: After I won a playwriting contest, as the grand prize I was able to spend a few weeks with the writing staff of *My Two Dads*. While I was there, I learned that they were looking for some story ideas. So, I asked the executive producer, Bob Myer, who was running the show at the time, if, after my gig was over, I could come in for a week or two to pitch some story ideas. Bob graciously agreed and I pitched an idea that he liked. They picked it up and paid me for it. Bob had a few of his writers write out the idea, and my first television credit was a story credit. After that, I was pretty much unemployed for about four years. It was a tough struggle. I wrote some freelance episodes on a children's television show called *Life with Louie*. I did a freelance episode that never got filmed for UPN's show *Sparks*. I also wrote a couple of sitcom pilots. Finally, my first full-time staff job came in 1997 on *Nash Bridges,* starring Don Johnson, and I wrote for three years on that show.

ALAN BALL: I wrote a play called *Five Women Wearing the Same Dress*, which is about bridesmaids in a big society wedding in Knoxville, Tennessee. I believe it was David Tockerman, who, at the time, was working for Carsey-Werner Television as basically a talent scout, who either read the play or saw the production. He asked for a meeting with me while he was in New York. At the time, I was new to the notion of meetings because I didn't really understand what they were all about. I met him in a hotel room, and that was 1992. Everyone was preoccupied with the '92 presidential election. Most of the meeting was spent discussing possible candidates, Ross Perot in particular. I left thinking, "That was strange. We didn't really talk about my writing, but I guess it went well." About a year and half later, I got offered a job writing for the sitcom *Grace Under Fire*. My first reaction was, "What is *Grace Under Fire,* anyway?" I didn't watch much television. Basically, I was a playwright living in New York City with a day job. After I came home from work, I was either concentrating on my own writing or in rehearsals doing some play in a basement theater somewhere. In particular, I didn't care about TV. So, I didn't know about any show, no less *Grace Under Fire*. It was a TV show about a Southern woman, and I think because my own play was about Southern women and was funny, they thought I could be a good fit to write for *Grace Under Fire*.

I went out to L.A. and met with the showrunner, Mark Flannigan, and got hired. I never really wanted nor expected to become a TV writer. I thought that because I was a playwright, I could make the transition to writing feature film scripts. I knew nothing about TV writing and the dynamics of being in a room with other writers. However, I reasoned, "How many times is this opportunity going to come my way?" From my experience at the theater company I was working at in New York, it was evident to me that most of the members, who I had previously known in college, thought of it as a hobby. For me, it was clear that being a professional writer was something I really wanted to do in my life. Most of the people in my theater group were focused on getting married and having families. I knew I was heading in a different direction. Writing on a sitcom was not the road I imagined, but what was the worst that could happen? I could end up hating it and move back to New York. No big deal. So, I moved to Los Angeles on a Friday and I started working on a Monday.

The Importance of Having a Mentor

AMY SHERMAN-PALLADINO: Bob Myer, who was running the *Roseanne* show while I was there, was a mentor to me in a lot of ways. I got to learn the "story breaking" technique from Bob. He was very generous and smart and never let his ego get in the way of the writing process. Bob taught me to be a real leader, to take that pencil and just GO! I've gone on to work with a lot of showrunners during my career where we have pitched ideas for hours and hours. The next thing you know it hits four in morning and you just want to scream, "So, pick one already!" Bob would never let us sit around for hours like that. He would take the pen himself, put his ass on the line, and create ideas and move forward. I never felt lost as a writer in that *Roseanne* writing room because of Bob Myer. *Roseanne* was a major learning experience. The writing was good and the "bar was set very high." I could not think of a better show to start my career on.

DENNIS LEONI: Probably the most influential mentor I've had is an executive producer named Gil Grant, whom I did three shows with. Initially, he hired me to write for an NBC show called *Hull High*. Then, he brought me on as an executive story editor on *Covington Cross,* which we shot in England. It was basically just like the show *Bonanza,* but set in the 1400s. I did another show with him called *McKenna,* which was about wilderness outfitters. Gil was responsible for teaching me the business and showing me how to function in a writers' room. He always told me that 75% of being a staff writer is getting along with the other writers. That's not always easy because there are a lot of personalities and egos in a writers' room. Everybody thinks that their idea is the best idea. It taught me a lot about writing and rewriting and how to make a story better. I consider Gil Grant my mentor.

MARK BRAZILL: Bonnie and Terry Turner are truly my mentors. They taught me everything. Terry Turner would sit in the editing room with me during the first season of *That '70s Show,* and I would observe everything he did. The Turners were great to me and I look up to them very much. They are a combination of wonderful producers and brilliant writers. After the first season of *That '70s Show,* they really let me run the program. It's really important to have somebody on your side like the Turners. They really protected me. The Turners felt I had a real vision for this show, and were extremely good about letting that come through, uninhibited. On *3rd Rock from the Sun,* I closely watched them work and learned a lot there, too. The Turners even got you home in time to eat dinner with your family, which I found fantastic. That's almost unheard of in this business. On some shows, the writers are working until four a.m. You watch the final result, and when it's really bad you then say to yourself, "What were they doing staying up all night?" In this regard, if the show is really bad, you can rationalize and say, "Yeah, but I was home for dinner." [Laughing] The Turners had the ability to write the joke themselves and move forward. They didn't sweat it and they didn't second-guess it. They are confident and talented writers.

TRACY GAMBLE: I worked for people who had written on some classic television shows—writers like Jack Allison, who had previously written for *The Andy Griffith Show*, and Dick Bensfield and Perry Grant, who had written every single episode of both the radio and TV series *Ozzie & Harriet*. These were tremendous talents to learn from and were real mentors for me. What I learned from Dick and Perry was a genuine work ethic. They would continually knock on our office doors and say, "I don't hear typewriters." They would come to work every day looking like they just stepped out of a JC Penny catalog. They wore business-like short-sleeve shirts, brought sack lunches, showed up in the morning at nine a.m. sharp, wrote till noon, took a lunch break, and then continued writing from one p.m. until five p.m., while all the time making sure everybody else was writing. I learned a work ethic from them, and for that I will be eternally grateful. I used to complain, "God, I am burned out!" They would reply, "What are you talking about? We wrote every episode of *Ozzie & Harriet* for radio!" It was a wonderful experience.

BRENDA HAMPTON: There were many different mentors in my life. First and foremost, it's important to work for good writers and producers, so you can learn the craft correctly. There's only one way to learn sitcom writing and that's to just do it. Early in my career, I worked on a show called *Blossom*. I really liked working for the showrunner, Don Reo, who has gone on to create *My Wife and Kids*. He was terrific and a mentor to me in a lot of ways. Later on in my career, Aaron Spelling became a mentor. Spelling is the executive producer of my show *7th Heaven*. During the first season, when I pitched stories to him, he guided me well. I could pitch four or five episodes at a time with four or five stories within each episode and he would listen to all of them. Then he would make very intelligent and knowledgeable suggestions on how to make it better. Spelling started his career as a playwright, so he really understands writers and is a wonderful man.

TOM FONTANA: I ended up staying on as a writer for *St. Elsewhere* for the run of the show. Bruce Paltrow eventually made me a producer. It was an extraordinary learning process. I went from being a guy who wrote plays that were performed in dark little spaces downtown and maybe seen by four people to writing a television show that was seen by millions of people. On a weekly basis, we were able to vent either our tragic spleen or our comic spleen. We tried to have a good mixture of both on the show. The other side of it was the enormous gift of having Bruce Paltrow as my teacher. He was a huge mentor for me in the sense that he was generous and also tough. So, when he said you wrote a good script, you actually went, "Wow, I wrote a good script!" He didn't coddle us at all. Bruce was available to really work with you, so you could truly understand the writing process. In addition to that, I was also at MTM [Mary Tyler Moore Productions] when they were making the transition from half-hour to hour shows. *Lou Grant* was already established and *Hill Street Blues* had been on for half a season. Being at MTM was like being at the Harvard University of the TV writers' world.

JONATHAN STARK: I would have to say that my boss at *Cheers,* Bill Steinkellner, was my mentor as far as improv goes. I learned writing through him because when you do improv, you learn the simplicity of staying on a subject and moving a story along, which is vitally important in writing. It's one of the main keys to writing a good script. Bill eventually hired me at *Cheers,* so everything came full-circle.

YVETTE LEE BOWSER: I would have to say that my mentor was Bill Cosby. I think I've learned to express myself through honest storytelling and storytelling with dignity. Those are values that Mr. Cosby instilled in me. I still have the ability to call him, but I don't necessarily do it because I don't want to be a pest. I feel that he was very generous in the first place in giving me the opportunity to enter into this business. Mr. Cosby opened a door for me, and I see that my responsibility is to open the door for others. He is a great man and a mentor in the truest sense of the word.

Creating Your Own Show

The Concept

LARRY DAVID: Jerry [Seinfeld] told me NBC wanted to do a show with him and asked me if I had any interest in working with him. We were splitting a cab across town, but before we got into the cab, we went into a grocery store to pick up some stuff. We started talking about the products in the store. It was the kind of conversation that you never heard on television between two friends. We both thought it contained the initial beginnings of a show, and that was the genesis of *Seinfeld.*

The origins of *Curb Your Enthusiasm* are a little bit different. After *Seinfeld* ended, Jeff Garlin, who plays my manager on the show, asked me what I was working on, and I told him that I was seriously thinking about going back into stand-up comedy after a 10-year hiatus. Jeff said, "You should film it." At first I was reluctant, but my wife and Jeff talked me into it. The question for me was, "What are they going to film?" I could visualize them filming when I am on-stage and maybe briefly off-stage, but what else are they going to see in this so-called documentary? I then thought I would probably have to make up some stuff so that we have a story going. Otherwise, I felt it would be terribly boring. So I wrote an outline, which required a wife, and I couldn't use my real wife, so I cast someone in the role. I then needed a manager and I asked Jeff to play the part. Of course, since it was supposed to be a documentary, it needed to be filmed like one. So, there couldn't be a script. It had to be improvised. At some point during the filming of this documentary, we realized it had potential to be a series.

DAVID KOHAN: We had a meeting with NBC and one of the things they told us was that *Mad About You* was going to be taken off the air. They were looking for a new "couple comedy." The reason we came up with *Will & Grace* was because we were always talking about love stories. One thing I learned from working for Sydney Pollack is that his movies were usually about love stories and that love stories sell. A love story is when a guy and girl kiss at the end, but a love story is only as good as the obstacles that keep them apart. At the end of a movie, the couple kiss and don't have to be apart anymore. In a television series, they have to be apart all the time to keep the audience interested. Max [Mutchnick] and I thought, "What is the real obstacle to keeping them apart?" We eventually came up with the idea that they will never get together because Will is gay. We also experienced that in our own lives. One of my closest friends was one of Max's closest friends and happened to be Max's ex-girlfriend. In high school, she thought that she and Max were going to get married. After college, Max came out, told her he was gay, and she really freaked out. Finally, when they came to terms with it, they developed this great friendship, even though in the back of both of their minds they instinctively knew they were ideally suited for one another. That seemed to me to be the basis for a romantic-comedy idea that we could play forever because the relationship could never be consummated.

JONATHAN STARK: When somebody mentioned Jim Belushi's name for a television pilot, I thought it could be interesting. I had seen a movie he was in called *Return to Me,* starring Bonnie Hunt, David Duchovny, and Minnie Driver. Jim played Bonnie Hunt's husband, a fairly small role, but I loved him in the part. I felt that this was a role he could play on television. I brought it up to my writing partner, Tracy [Newman], and she said, "I think Jim is kind of sexy." We decided to meet with him. Disney liked the idea.

Our executive producer, Suzanne Bukinik, was major in getting this show on the air. Suzanne was an executive at ABC before she became our partner. Tracy and I had an outline in our heads about the show, but Suzanne gave us notes and support that helped us to define the idea more solidly in our minds. The outline focused on who this character was and his outlook on life. Then we pitched it to NBC.

BARBARA HALL: The concept for *Joan of Arcadia* came about while I was doing *Judging Amy,* a show I developed for CBS. I was running *Judging Amy* and happy doing it. I thought the only thing that would make me want to leave *Judging Amy* would be something really out there, extremely creative and something that would scare me to do. I had written an episode of *Chicago Hope* in which Peter MacNicol comes back from the dead during a hallucination sequence. As a result, he's able to answer questions about the afterlife. It was so much fun to do, rooted in a certain kind of reality and also funny. It was like the voice from beyond that you would want to hear that was personable, and Peter, of course, made it that way. I really enjoyed doing that episode and thought it would be great to do a show like that every week where somebody gets to talk to God. I've also had a life-long interest in Joan of Arc as a female icon. She is the person I identified with as a little girl because being a Southern Protestant I was fascinated by Catholic icons. At the time, I also had a pre-teen daughter and I was just sort of musing about what it would look like if a teenage girl were asked to have that kind of calling and if she would be willing to do it.

MARK BRAZILL: *3rd Rock from the Sun* was produced by Carsey-Werner Productions. They asked Bonnie and Terry Turner to create a show with the theme being the decade of the 1970s. Bonnie and Terry told the partners, Marcy

Carsey and Tom Werner, that they wanted to do the show with me, because they liked me and we all got along great.

The Turners really jumpstarted my career. I also think that succeeding in this business has a lot to do with luck. Many people who are very talented have good scripts that don't go anywhere. Unfortunately, it just doesn't happen for them. I was always in the right spot at the right time.

ILENE CHAIKEN: The concept for *The L Word* originated with my writing an article for *Los Angeles* magazine. I am not a journalist, nor have I done any journalistic writing. Our children were two years old, and I was kind of taken by the number of gay people I knew who were starting families. I had a group of friends who were either adopting children, giving birth to children, or contemplating starting families. All of a sudden, gay men were doing it in large numbers. I saw it as a real phenomenon. I told my agent about it, and he hooked me up with an editor at *Los Angeles* magazine. I told the editor some stories about the subject, and she told me to write the piece. I wrote this rather long essay piece in 1999, and it was the forerunner of all of the articles that have surfaced in the last couple of years on this subject. This was just at the very beginning of recognizing this as a cultural phenomenon. Anyway, I wrote this magazine article and I realized I was writing stories about my life and the lives of people I've known. There were a lot of wonderful stories, and it was not just about gay people having babies. It was just simply about the stories of our lives in a way in which they hadn't been told. That is what made me want to do it, and as I started thinking more, it was apparent that it should be a television series.

BILL LAWRENCE: My creating the concept for *Scrubs* is interesting. I was trying to think of a show to write about and a couple of important things happened. Developmentally, the TV landscape had evolved to a point where there were so many more shows on the air. Therefore, there was greater competition to hook the audience, whether it was via heart or depth. The challenge to create a show where people really care about the characters was greater than ever. The important prototype shows for me were *M*A*S*H* and *The Wonder Years,* because they were both shows that combined comedy and depth.

My best friend from college is a guy named J.D. He was an overall "screw-up." In my fraternity in college, he was a good-time kind of guy. Somehow, some way, he asserted himself and is now a doctor. In fact, he is a cardiologist. J.D. is also the medical advisor on the show. J.D. and two other friends of mine who I grew up with became doctors. When we would all get together to drink beers and talk, one common thread they all mentioned was how overwhelming their internship and residency was. I remember J.D. saying to me that everyone remembers that first horrible and terrifying day they experience on a new job, no matter what the job is. Everyone wants to do well. Now, imagine that pressure multiplied by 1,000% because you have to take care of people, and whether or not they live or die depends on you. I thought it was a great basis for a story.

Something that I would like to point out is that one of the great aspects about *M*A*S*H,* and why I still love it so much, is that nowadays all of our medical shows are dramas. I think that's because we want our doctors to be serious, dramatic, and heroic. Anyone who has a friend who's a doctor will probably agree with me that even though that person is a doctor, he or she still has a sense of humor. They are still goofy at certain times. That person can also be insecure and vulnerable. So, I thought this could be a very interesting idea to play off of.

I basically hit up my buddy J.D. and all of his doctor friends for stories. All of the medical stories we do on our show are true. One of the cool things is that from those original doctors, we met five more doctors. From those five doctors, we met five more, and so on, and so on. We spend every hiatus interviewing doctors to get a bunch of new stories. We never make up the medical stuff or any of the patient stories on *Scrubs.* They are all pulled from real life. You know about the old cliché of going to a cocktail party, meeting a doctor, and saying, "Oh, my arm hurts." Well, for all of us who write on *Scrubs,* when we are out at a dinner party or a bar, especially in Los Angeles, and a doctor finds out that we are writers on the show, they always say, "I have the funniest story and you guys have got to use it!" We are very big in the medical community. [Laughing] NBC was nice enough to let me do *Scrubs* as a single-camera show and with no laugh track. I wanted to do a show that was really broad. I wanted it to be silly and goofy and also serious, all in the same half-hour.

SHAWN RYAN: The idea for *The Shield* was really comprised of three or four different ideas that got thrown into the same pot. I began to think about the concept during my third season of *Nash Bridges,* which was technically a cop show of much lighter fare. I was a big fan of *NYPD Blue, Homicide,* and *Law & Order,* but there was not a new cop show on the air at that time which truly excited me. So, I just started thinking about a cop show that I would be motivated to want to watch. The first thing I thought about was what a cop show would look like on HBO. *NYPD Blue* was so good. However, there were some episodes where Sipowicz would throw some guy against a wall and say, "You dirt bag," when you knew he really wanted to say, "You shit head!" So, I began to wonder what that would all look like. Also, in doing research for *Nash Bridges,* I went on a couple of police "ride-alongs" with detectives in San Francisco, and I began to get a sense of cop culture that had a dark edge and dark humor to it. I definitely didn't see a lot of that on the existing TV cop shows. On most of the shows, the cops were honest, earnest, and always trying to do the right thing. They would never make inappropriate jokes over dead bodies, for instance. This is essentially what I saw up in San Francisco. Part of my inspiration was to get that dynamic into a TV show.

I began to write some scenes and they were okay, but still not where I wanted them to be. However, what really crystallized the concept was, when I was writing the pilot for *The Shield,* a major scandal broke in the Rampart Division of the Los Angeles Police Department. I began to read all of these articles in the newspaper about how there seemed to be a whole squad of detectives and officers that had kind of ignored a lot of the rules and laws. They appeared to become a Wild West police force of their own in the Rampart area of Los Angeles. Awful allegations were being thrown around. Today, people don't know which allegations were true and which weren't, but at the time, it was fascinating to me. What really interested me about the story was that you would read on one page of the newspaper about these terrible allegations and then, on another page, you would read that crime was down all over the country—even specifically in that area of Los Angeles. When these free-wheeling crash units at Rampart were really at their height of power, crime was definitely down. The cops seemed to be effective even if their methods were deemed unacceptable.

At the time, I had just had a baby girl with my wife, and it was our first child. I started having all of these disaster fantasies of bad things that could happen to my daughter. I couldn't help but imagine all of these horrible things in the world that could happen to her. I started thinking and putting it together with this Rampart Division scandal. I thought to myself, "Gee, how would I want the cops to act if it was my daughter in danger? How much of a stickler for the laws would I be? Or, would I want the cops to bend the laws to help keep my daughter safe?" So, I started to have a philosophical debate in my own head about what I would want done. It's a really hard question, and yet I knew that if you allow an officer to bend the rules when it is convenient for you, then they are going to start breaking the laws when it is convenient for them. It's a very slippery slope. I realized that I not only wanted to make a cop show about good cops, but I wanted to make it about the bad cops, too. I wanted to write about what makes them bad. Then I began to think about questions like: Are there times when we want the cops to be bad? Are their times when we ignore the cops being bad as long as they are doing the dirty work for us? At night, when my daughter was sleeping, I would write down notes literally in the room that she was sleeping in. One of the major plot points in the pilot for *The Shield* is that there is a little girl who is missing. In the episode, the police kind of exhausted the ways to find her and they sort of allowed Vic Mackey to get rough with a suspect to find out where this little girl is. That kind of aggression by Mackey to find the answers came from the central question I was asking about and the honest concern I have for my own daughter.

TOM FONTANA: The idea for *Oz* started in my mind a long time ago. When I was in college, the riots happened in Attica Prison, which is not too far from my hometown of Buffalo. It was brutal from the standpoint of the riots themselves and to the actions of the National Guard coming in and killing people. It was a terrible event in our history. That incident stuck with me. I asked myself, "What did the prisoners mean when they said it was bad there? Isn't it supposed to always be bad in prison? After all, they are prisoners. Prison is where the Joker went after Batman clobbered him." The more that I heard about the things that were going on at Attica, the more I got intrigued. Then, when I was doing *Homicide,* every week or so in our script, we would send someone to prison. At the end of a broadcast cop show, the crook goes to jail, and that is the history of television. We are happy at the end of an episode of *Homicide* when the murderer gets caught and is sent away. But, that is not the end of the story. So, it all made me think. I started wondering what happens after they are sent away to prison. At the time, HBO was looking for an hour-long drama, but they didn't know what they were looking for. Sheila Nevins, who is the head of their documentary division, had a lot of success doing prison documentaries. Therefore, they were more open to my idea. HBO didn't really have an agenda. They weren't trying to fit a slot between *Friends* and *ER.* HBO basically had the attitude, "Let's give it a try."

J.J. ABRAMS: The first TV show that I created, *Felicity,* was about sweet, loving young people in college. It was ultimately such a tame show that it began to frustrate me. There weren't any further avenues of story coming into play. The fundamental thing you need for a long-running series is external forces coming in and testing your main characters. *Felicity* didn't have much of that, mostly because college, by definition, is a starting place of exploration and experimentation of failures, successes, relationships, love, and heartbreak. There are no real stakes in that, since you're supposed to take risks and to experiment at that stage of life. That isn't bad for 30, 40, 60, 70 hours of story. When you get to hour 80 and you don't really have bad guys, criminals, and disease to use as fodder for your story, it becomes very difficult. *Alias* was something I wanted to do because it felt like it was a show that would give me all the things that I would need to create those kinds of stories and also let me do all the stuff that I loved doing on *Felicity.* I came up with the idea for *Alias* and pitched it to the network. I told them it is the story of a young woman who was a spy and discovers her life is not what it seems to be. She finds that her only ally is her father, with whom she is estranged. They liked the idea and I wrote the pilot.

YVETTE LEE BOWSER: This is how I created my first show, *Living Single*. Warner Brothers and The Fox Network had talent-holding deals with Kim Coles and Queen Latifah, and they were looking for someone to come up with an idea that would feature those two ladies. I just thought that my girlfriends and I and the four personalities that live inside of me are pretty entertaining. That was where *Living Single* was derived from. I did not pitch another concept. Latifah and Kim were pretty aggressive in wanting the studio and networks to give an opportunity to someone of color to write something for them. This was partly because they had both been involved in failed pilots written by people who were not of color. I think that they felt that if they were going to try again, they should at least give an opportunity to someone who was more culturally plugged into their voices.

I was a writer/producer on *Hangin' with Mr. Cooper* at that time and more than ready to leave there. It was a very oppressive environment on that show. Basically, they didn't dig female writers, and that was very different from my wonderful experience on *A Different World*. I earned the right to be heard on that show. When I was not given the chance to be heard on *Hangin' with Mr. Cooper,* I said to myself, "If this is what most of Hollywood is like, I will not last very long. I don't have the patience for it." So, I thought instead of getting mad, I would dig in and get to work. Then, I pursued development earnestly, and that was when the opportunity of creating *Living Single* was brought to me. I ran with it! We caught lightning in a bottle with the pilot. Then, the show became popular and was the number one show in African-American and Latino households for the five years it was on the air. I am very proud of that.

JOSS WHEDON: I came up with the idea for *Buffy* largely due to my fascination with horror movies where the girl always gets killed. I identify with female victims who have been mugged. Most of my work is in gender studies, so I am interested in subjects on women and particularly women as heroes. I wasn't seeing them in television. So, I wanted to take that victim character and turn it on its ear. I wanted to give her some fun. It wasn't even going to be *Buffy the Vampire Slayer*. The vampire angle was kind of irrelevant in a way. The story was more about a girl who no one takes seriously, but has incredible responsibility and power.

When I created my latest show, *Angel*, the concept occurred to me in three stages. One stage was that the *Angel* character from *Buffy* was really popping, and sooner or later we are going to run out of stories of what to do with him. The second stage was the episode entitled "I Only Have Eyes for You," where David Boreanaz showed me he could really act extremely well. Boreanaz did very subtle, interesting work, and I thought, "I have a star here." The third stage was realizing that there was another story here about a different element, concerning redemption and past mistakes. The difficulty and moral mutability in searching for redemption for what you've done in the past is not an adolescent story at all. That was when I said, "We have a show. I have a star and he has a name and I have a reason to go somewhere else."

BRENDA HAMPTON: I came up with the idea for *7th Heaven* rather quickly. I was working an excruciating number of hours on the sitcom *Mad About You*. At that time, an agent called me and asked if I wanted to pitch a family show to the legendary television producer Aaron Spelling. I thought, "Dear diary, today I met Aaron Spelling." I quickly answered, "Yes, I definitely want to go for that meeting." [Laughing] That Sunday night before the Monday meeting with Spelling, I started with the idea of *7th Heaven* and finished it up during my drive from Sony Tri-Star to the Spelling building. *7th Heaven* was loosely based on a minister I knew in New York. Then I created the other characters mostly from my imagination, but also from other people I knew. In essence, I just created a family.

DENNIS LEONI: I have to credit my wife, Debbie, in helping me come up with the idea of *Resurrection Blvd.* She told me years ago that a real wave of Latino programming is going to happen someday. I'm a mixture of Mexican and Italian heritage, and Debbie felt that I needed to write about the Latino part of my cultural background. I wrote a script called *La Reforma,* which was, basically, my "Wonder Years" growing up in Tucson, Arizona. It was about my family. It had some edge, because it dealt with my grandfather's alcoholism. But, overall it is a sweet story. I knew Jerry Offsay, who was the president of Showtime, and he wanted to develop a Latino family drama. So, I gave him *La Reforma.* Showtime read it and told me they loved the writing, but the show was not right for them. They then asked me to rethink it. I came home and I began watching Showtime. A boxing match was on with two Latino fighters. Then it dawned on me. Latino, boxing, Showtime—they all seemed like a natural fit. I then married the family drama to the boxing aspect. The boxing gave us that whole dark underbelly and some action. It was also great because it became a metaphor for a Latino family literally fighting for a piece of the American dream.

The Pitch Process

TRACY GAMBLE: I was writing on *According to Jim* and I felt I was a major part of the show, but I also felt it was time to broaden my horizons and expand my résumé. I basically said to my agents at United Talent Agency, "Get me a pilot." My agents said, "There is a book called *8 Simple Rules for Dating My Teenage Daughter* written by W. Bruce Cameron and they want to turn it into a television series. Maybe you should read it." Well, I took a look at this book and I quickly realized that I was definitely the person for this job. In the book, there are two teenage daughters and a teenage son, and I happen to have two teenage daughters and a teenage son.

The book was owned by executive producers Tom Shadyac and Michael Bostick. Since they are essentially movie people, the agency teamed them up with television producer Flody Suarez. Flody called me in for a meeting. He asked, "What did you think of the book?" I replied, "I didn't read the book because my daughter came in and did this and this and this, and my son came in and did that and that and that." They all started laughing. They honestly understood that basically I couldn't read it because I had just experienced a horrific weekend with my own daughters and son. They then announced, "You're the guy to write this show!"

That day, my eldest daughter, Bridget, came in the house and said, "I made a date with this guy for the prom and I really want to go with this other guy." I said, "No, you have to honor your commitment." Later, my other daughter, Kerry, came in, and she was just being a total pain in the ass. I then said to Bridget, "You are honoring your commitment and that is final." Then, I said to my other daughter, "You are not going to the dance. You are grounded!" She replied, "Fine, because nobody asked me anyway." I muttered to myself, "Oh, God!" A lot of this series comes from my life, and many of the experiences with the children come from my own children's lives. Actually, the pilot episode is based on the book as well as experiences from my own life with my children.

AMY SHERMAN-PALLADINO: Susan Daniel, the head of The WB, asked to meet with me. We would always have these great meetings, but Susan would inevitably ask me to write an hour-long show. I was essentially a half-hour comedy writer, not an hour writer. At the same time, I was coming off writing for *Veronica's Closet* and I was burned out and unemployed. I was feeling like I couldn't go through that half-hour grind anymore. My husband was working and he said, "Take some time off to write something else." So, I went straight back to The WB and we began talking about ideas.

The idea for *Gilmore Girls* was not even the idea I originally wanted to do. I pitched an idea for a show involving a Filipino girl, a very involved plot. After the pitch, I threw out a few other ideas and one of them was about a mother and daughter who are best friends—more like real, genuine pals than mother and daughter. They said, "That's what we want. Great. Now, go write it!" I originally thought of it as a half-hour show, and they said, "How about making it an hour-long show?" I thought to myself, "Does that just involve more paper?"

After I sold it, I walked out of the meeting and realized that I had just sold a sentence, not a show. I said to myself, "I don't know who my characters are or where they live. I don't know anything about them."

Although pitching a concept is very exhausting, it's actually one of my strengths. From my personal experience, you are never going to walk out of a pitch meeting with anybody truly understanding what you just pitched them. They are often not listening because of various and understandable reasons, such as: they have a lunch appointment at one p.m.; they have to go to a doctor's appointment; they have four other shows that are falling apart; they have an agent they have to deal with, and so on. They are giving me maybe 10% of their attention. So, the pitch process is really selling yourself and not the product. My experience is that you must walk into a room and essentially say through your pitch: "Look how crazy, funny, and fun I am. If I'm this nuts, imagine what I can give you on paper." [Laughing] It's all about selling your confidence. You are basically saying, "Look how much fun you're having right now. Imagine how much fun everyone else will have tuning into my show every week."

LARRY DAVID: The pitching of *Seinfeld* was very similar to the episode we did where Jerry and George are pitching their sitcom, which is essentially about "nothing." We were telling the executives our ideas and we told them it was a one-camera show. NBC saw it as a three-camera show. I told them that's not what this show is about. I remember getting some very strange looks from the Castle Rock executives who were in the room when, like George, I said, "This is not the show." Anyway, I eventually submitted to the multi-camera format.

For *Curb Your Enthusiasm*, it was, again, pitched as a documentary of me going back to do stand-up after a 10-year hiatus. The day we pitched it, HBO bought it as a special right there in the room. When we finished the documentary, Chris Albrecht at HBO approached me about doing it as a series.

YVETTE LEE BOWSER: When I pitched *Living Single* to the network, it wasn't tough for me because, at that time in my career, I had nothing to lose and everything to gain. At one point, there was a female character named Maxine Shaw who happened to be very aggressive and sexual, but at the same time, very confident with her sexuality, her strengths, and her knowledge. With the first draft of the pilot script, I felt that a lot of the male executives were very threatened by her. They wanted me to take that character completely out of the show. Again, not knowing any better I said, "Taking Max out of the show is like taking a part of me out of the show and I won't do it!" I then came up with a creative compromise that worked for me. This was to take her out of the brownstone where the other three women lived and to move her across the street. I then got some more comedy out of it because she didn't live there, but she was always hanging out there. It gave the show another dimension and it also distinguished the characters better. It lessened her presence a bit in the pilot episode, but she still stayed in the series. The character of Max was brilliantly played by Erika Alexander, and she won three NAACP Image Awards for that role.

BARBARA HALL: It was not tough to pitch the network on the initial idea of *Joan of Arcadia*, but it did take three years of gestation from the time it occurred to me to the time that anyone would validate my parking, let alone buy the idea. Originally, I wasn't going to take it to CBS. I didn't think it was their kind of show. But I had talked about it to so many people that CBS got wind of it and wanted it. In a weird way, I pre-sold it. CBS had a very straightforward development slate, so they were looking for the show that was going to be their offbeat show and I won.

BILL LAWRENCE: It was a little tough pitching the network on the idea for *Scrubs*. I wrote the pilot when I was working for ABC. I gave it to them and they had no interest, whatsoever. So, it now is on NBC, but it is actually owned by ABC, which is really weird. Basically, the script was around for a year until somebody at NBC said they felt it would be fun to do. It wasn't that hard to pitch the network on the idea. I just thought it would never happen that the network would buy into it, to tell you the truth. That part of the process was tough for me.

BRENDA HAMPTON: I didn't really come into my pitch meeting with Aaron Spelling to sell *7th Heaven*. I actually came in to meet the legendary TV producer Aaron Spelling. I didn't put that much pressure on myself. However, by the same token, I did not want to make a fool of myself, either. I wanted it to be a solid pitch. I wasn't primarily concerned with selling the show. I just wanted to make a good impression and meet Aaron Spelling.

Spelling made me feel very comfortable in the room and showed he's such a dear, dear man. He pulled up a chair knee-to-knee with me and said, "Okay, kid, what do you got?" I had a great time pitching the show, and I sold *7th Heaven* in the room with him. I then went over to Jonathan Levin's office at Spelling Television. We called The WB network and I sold it to them.

I'm not a performer. I'm a writer. So, I do not necessarily enjoy going into pitch meetings. I'd rather give my ideas to someone on paper. I guess that at this point in my career, I have pitched so many things that the pitch process doesn't make me feel as uncomfortable anymore.

DENNIS LEONI: On my show *Resurrection Blvd.,* the pitch process with Showtime was terrific. The network had already read and understood the family part. So, I basically said, "Here is the full deal. We have the perfect mix of boxing, Showtime, and Latinos." They immediately understood it, because they had all of these Latin fighters already under contract at Showtime. I pitched them the story of how the family suffers a setback and halts their dream to have a boxing champion. Then, the other younger brother steps up to the challenge.

The pitch process is definitely a difficult process. I know most of the executives fairly well at this point. We usually have a nice chat before we head into a business discussion, because I don't like to just jump into things immediately at a meeting. I like to go in there and tell them a little about the story and where it comes from. Yes, the pitch process can be a pain because odds are they are not going to buy it. It is difficult to sell a show because you have got a hundred different people meeting with the network every year, pitching thousands of projects. The odds are not very good that they'll pick your idea. Obviously, the better the track record you bring to the table, the better your chances are of a sale. You just pray that the executive you are dealing with has a sensibility that will allow him or her to see what you want to do. Since I have always done projects that are a little different and not of the ordinary, it doesn't make my task easier. The networks always tell you that they want something different, but they always wind up making the same doctor, lawyer, cop drama shows. It's maddening! Executives get scared to take chances because they are worried about losing their jobs. However, the real truth is that the ones who do take chances usually end up moving up the ladder.

JOSH SCHWARTZ: I met with Stephanie Savage, who runs Wonderland Productions, which is director McG's company. [McG helmed the two *Charlie's Angels* movies.] Wonderland had seen and liked a show I had written, and for which a pilot was shot for The WB, called *Wall to Wall Records.* This unfortunately did not go to series. Stephanie Savage and I began talking about the overview of *The O.C.,* which was from a Newport Beach standpoint, where a lot of the kids from USC are from. Because of that, I felt I had a pretty good view of that aspect of the "Newport Beach world," especially from an outsider's perspective. I also felt it was an interesting world that hadn't been explored on television. We spoke about where they wanted the show to go and what they wanted it, generally, to be about. I left and then came back with the characters written and flushed out. The whole thing evolved from there. For me, the character of Seth and the Cohen family in *The O.C.* was very much like my experience from USC. Seth's dynamic with his dad is very much reminiscent of my dynamic with my own father. A lot of the parent stories are more about my life growing up on the East Coast. But, of course, I transform the stories to the West Coast because Newport Beach, in particular, is much more affluent and the people have a lot better tans.

DAVID KOHAN: When we went in to pitch NBC, we originally pitched another pilot script to them with the characters of Will and Grace as ancillary characters within a bigger ensemble cast. It was NBC that really thought that these characters Will and Grace should be the focal point of the show. We actually didn't want to pitch Will and Grace as the central couple because we felt that NBC would get scared off since *Ellen* had gone down the year before. The "coming out" *Ellen* episode was the highlight for that show the year before. The basis of the series for the next season was Ellen as a gay woman. The show did not succeed based on that new approach. However, NBC didn't care about that, they just wanted a show based around these two characters Will and Grace. It goes to show that when you go in to pitch a network, they may see something that you as a writer may not even see yourself in your own script.

ILENE CHAIKEN: I very casually pitched the concept [of *The L Word*] to some folks whom I was working with at Showtime. This was long before I wrote the pilot. I pitched it as an ensemble drama about lesbians. This was before *Queer as Folk, Will & Grace*, and *Queer Eye for the Straight Guy*. Showtime didn't laugh at me when I pitched the idea. However, it was kind of understood that this was a radical idea and that nobody was going to touch it, not even a premium cable network. But, I presented it to them and gave them a couple of pages that consisted of some stories and characters that I was interested in developing further. The two women whom I pitched it to said, "We love this. It is great and really intriguing. But, I don't think the guys are going to get it. The guys are the ones who will ultimately have to say yes." Then everything changed in television. There was the advent of gay television, and all of a sudden, these programs over the last year or two began getting a great deal of attention. *Queer as Folk* also proved to be successful for Showtime. The night that my first movie that I wrote for Showtime, *Dirty Pictures*, won the Golden Globe, Jerry Offsay, who was the president of Showtime, came up to me at the Golden Globe Awards ceremony and whispered in my ear, "We are going to develop that lesbian show with you."

Writing the Pilot

BRENDA HAMPTON: *7th Heaven* has now been on the air eight seasons. When I originally pitched the characters, each character truly had their own story. So, at that stage, it was a matter of just sitting down and blending the stories together. I don't think the process of writing that original pilot was actually much different from the way I write now.

When you think of a story, it has a beginning, a middle, and an end. It also has some twists and turns to it, but, essentially, it's comprised of those three parts. Also, when writing the pilot, I wanted it to be true to the family genre because that was what the network was looking to produce at that time. Looking back, writing the pilot was not a difficult process. When I turned in the script, I did not receive a lot of notes from the network, and I think by the third draft I had what the network wanted to produce.

JOSH SCHWARTZ: I think it is important to write a pilot that sets up scenarios that go beyond the first episode. This way, the show ultimately has legs on it. To be honest, that is the hardest part of the process. I had written a few pilots before *The O.C.* Looking back, I would have been dead if one of those shows went to series. [Laughing] It can be a great pilot, but it doesn't mean the show can develop into a great series. I think *The O.C.* pilot was about building as many relationships that could interact and grow as much as possible. Granted, the setup and teaming up of as many different characters as possible is important. However, you also must have the story land, emotionally. The challenge is twofold. If you really believe in the father-son relationship between Sandy and Seth Cohen, and in the brotherly friendship bond between Seth and Ryan, then these relationships can grow emotionally. Therefore, I felt that this show had the potential to work. On top of that, since we had both the adult world and the kid world to work with, we knew it could provide us with a lot of material for future episodes. There were many storylines in the pilot. The story of Ryan coming to town was one storyline. The story of a woman not marrying her high-school sweetheart, but now finding herself living next door to that same guy, and the choices they made, was another storyline. In fact, that could have been its very own show. So, we had strong enough storylines underneath the umbrella of this show. There was definitely depth. Also, we knew that Ryan would be the eyes for the audience into this world. I felt it was absolutely essential that this world be fascinating enough via Ryan's perspective. If it was, then the show could succeed. It was important, according to network considerations, that the adult characters remain an important element of the show. In fact, that was also a path that I very much wanted to follow anyway. When we sold the show, we spoke a lot about movies like *The Ice Storm* starring Kevin Kline and Sigourney Weaver. That film was as much about the lives of the kids as it was about the adults.

One of the things we were very careful about doing in *The O.C.* was not making a statement in any way. We had a lot of drinking and drug use by the teens in the pilot, and we didn't want to send a message one way or another. We just wanted to represent the events in as real a way as possible and let people draw their own conclusions, based on that. I knew that down the line, I did not want to make it a show about "Who is addicted to what this week?" or, "Who is ODing this week?" It was something we knew that would get old and routine very quickly. The two main characters shared a cigarette in the pilot, and I thought that would be a firestorm of controversy, but it really wasn't.

ILENE CHAIKEN: I worked on writing the pilot for *The L Word* over the course of a year. In writing the pilot, I was drawing upon two decades of stories and life experience. There are two characters in *The L Word* whom I channel through and reflect the way I stand in the world. They are also completely different from me and are not me. Also, the two characters are from two very different periods of my life. The character of Jenny is from 25 years ago, but I made her a contemporary character with modern issues that are a little different from mine. She is a young writer dealing with her sexuality, dealing with coming out, and dealing with breaking her boyfriend's heart because she realizes that she might perhaps prefer to be with women. The other character is Bette, who is the driven, focused, alpha character who has a lot of these issues, who supports her family and takes everything on in that way. The reason I think these two characters really are the anchor of the show is because I take a stand in the real world from these two points of view.

MARK BRAZILL: Bonnie and Terry Turner and I got together to write the pilot for *That '70s Show*. The pilot script was going to consist of a total of 21 scenes. We divided the 21 scenes between us, and we wrote seven scenes apiece. Then, after we wrote our individual scenes, we brought all of the scenes together. Terry, Bonnie, and I worked closely to punchup the jokes, and basically we rewrote the pilot script as a team. When that process was finished, we had the final product for the pilot. The great thing about the Turners is not only are they very talented writers, but they are also extremely fast writers. So, the process was a real joy and a wonderful learning experience.

AMY SHERMAN-PALLADINO: After selling the pitch to The WB, I went on vacation to New York with my husband and we drove to Connecticut. It was the first time in my life I had never been to Connecticut. We stayed at this very charming inn called The Mayflower. I couldn't stop thinking that this whole place was right out of a movie. It was so "central casting" in the sense that it was October and the leaves were changing to these beautiful colors and there were signs around that read "Pumpkin Patch." The church on Sunday morning was packed. You go to the local diner and everyone knew each other. It was very idyllic and perfect for the *Gilmore Girls'* setting. I literally woke up one morning and said to myself, "She will live in Stars Hollow, Connecticut." That morning, I wrote some of the dialogue that actually wound up in the pilot. It just sort of happened and it felt good.

DAVE HACKEL: I wrote the pilot script for *Becker* with a special character in mind. This was a character that I really liked. I was at the point where I wanted to write something politically incorrect. When you write for network television for a living, you have a lot of harnesses on you. For example, a network might say, "You can't do that at 8:00 p.m. It is way too racy." Or, they might say, "Those types of characters are not acceptable because they're not nice." However, when you look around at the shows you've really loved, they have elements of all those things. Archie Bunker said horrible things to people. He was a stupid, uneducated man. But, there was a heart underneath Archie Bunker, and people realized that as time went on. So, when I was creating John Becker, I picked qualities of characters from shows that I liked and then picked parts of me, and even parts of other people. I wanted to have a character who spoke exactly what was on his mind. There was no filter.

I sat down and wrote the pilot, and afterwards I felt it was an episode of something I would like to watch on television. During the writing of the pilot, I was having lunch with two friends of mine at Paramount and asked them, "What do you guys think of my lead character being a doctor?" They said, "Sure, that could work." I then went back to my office and wrote a scene with him as a doctor that actually stayed in the pilot. The scene is when Becker is examining a very overweight patient and says to him, "I looked at all your test results and I looked over your physical and I have only one word for you. Salad! This is ridiculous! I'm sure you have a wife and kid who love you, and if you don't love yourself, I'm sure they do. So, take care of yourself. Don't be a jerk!" No one had ever told the fat guy he is, in fact, *fat*. Becker wanted to give him a dose of tough love. That was the kind of doctor he was. There was no gray area. He told him you are too fat and you will die. The patient got the message. The patient might not like him, but what are you looking for in a doctor, a new best friend? Or are you seeking a medical professional who can save your life?

YVETTE LEE BOWSER: I inherited the concept of *Half & Half*. It was a defunct script in development at CBS four years ago. I was given the script with free reign to rewrite it and cast it with African-American talent. It was originally written with Caucasian actors in mind. I did a rewrite, which wasn't actually a rewrite to make it more ethnic. It was just meant to clean up the story and make the characters more dimensional. I saw it as a wonderful writing experiment, to maintain the integrity of the original script, not simply add dialogue that might be more culturally specific. This kind of proved my point that writing is writing. When I am writing, I am not just writing characters of color. I am writing for people. I am telling human stories, not just black stories.

According to the Writers Guild, I did not create the show *Half & Half*. However, I certainly breathed life into it! I developed *Half & Half* and I am the surrogate mother in a sense. The person who wrote the original script is not involved with the show at all. So, all of the storylines beyond the pilot script have come from me and my staff. A great deal of texture for the series has come from my personal life. I have a half-sister that I didn't grow up with who is now living with me. I wasn't given a bible of stories or direction to follow for seasons to come. I was just given a script that I needed to put some "more meat on," and I ran with it. Essentially, it is my show.

BARBARA HALL: It took me three years of just thinking about the idea for *Joan of Arcadia*. Although I didn't realize it at the time, having read a lot of theology and physics books helped inspire this as an interest of mine. I was reading and studying these subjects on an ongoing basis. By the time I got ready to do the show, I had all of this knowledge of world religions and physics, which was very helpful.

The actual writing of the pilot for *Joan of Arcadia* was just a normal process. The odd thing about it was that when I was halfway through writing the pilot, I realized I had no real idea what the series was all about and I shouldn't even finish writing the pilot. I thought about calling CBS and saying, "I just don't know what this show is, so let's not even bother." Then, I had a change of heart. I decided halfway through that what happens to the show after I finish the pilot is not really my business. My business was to finish this pilot. So, that is what I did, and it wound up having a life of its own.

Putting Yourself in the Characters You Create

MARK BRAZILL: With the character of Eric Forman [played by Topher Grace] on *That '70s Show,* I have tried to put as many personal things as I could into him. Jackie and Jeff Filgo, who are executive producers on the show, have put in as many true stories as they could from their own lives. It seems that the show works better if stories for the episodes are built on something from real life, as opposed to some kind of made-up situation. I was never a big fan of focusing on the consequences and morals in a story. That is not how real life is. You sometimes get away with stuff, and sometimes you don't do anything but still get blamed for it. Life is just messy and unpredictable like that.

TRACY GAMBLE: Well, first of all, John Ritter and I got along great. He was really funny and a truly wonderful actor. It was fun to write for him. If you look at movies in John Ritter's career, like *Slingblade,* you will see that he can easily take a dark, dramatic turn in a role. Although, even when he is in a dramatic role, he can do that little Ritter turn of the head, and it can make you laugh. What actually is me in the Paul Hennessy character in *8 Simple Rules* is that I want to be a good father and a good husband, but I fear I'm not. I think that's what I brought to the writing of this character.

ALAN BALL: As far as the lead character, Lester Burnham, whom I created in the film *American Beauty* and was played brilliantly by Kevin Spacey, it is mostly autobiographical. It is about a man who has lost his passion. I was 42, myself, when the movie was made. There was a lot of flirting with mid-life and thinking that maybe there was less time ahead of me than there was behind me. I was compelled to think about all those choices I made. Was this where I wanted my life to be? That's what interested me about Lester Burnham. It's a fairly spiritual movie. The film is about these themes: "What are our lives about in a culture where we work to amass things and where, basically, all our daily cultural messages are pretty hollow? Where do we find the meaning in our lives?" I think that Lester knows he is looking for meaning and he foolishly misdirects it toward this young high-school girl. At least, he is looking and searching, as opposed to his wife, who I think is a very tragic character. She seems to have just given up. I think that happens to a lot of people, which is horrible. These are issues you do not see in a lot of movies. I don't consciously recall thinking that this is the theme I wanted to tackle, because then it feels like a term paper. For me, writing is more of a kind of blind groping in the dark. I trust my own instincts. In retrospect, looking back to the work that has been the most meaningful to me, I think thematically that I like examining the notion of how it's becoming more and more difficult to lead an authentic life. This is chiefly because the world is becoming more and more synthetic and transparent.

YVETTE LEE BOWSER: I absolutely put myself in the characters that I create. Some of the more intelligent, esoteric, silly, and superficial things that these characters say are all things that I have at least thought of at some point in my life. So, I can articulate those thoughts through these characters. I guess I get to hide a lot. [Laughing] It is a lot of fun to be able to express myself through all the characters that I have created over the years.

SHAWN RYAN: I would think, considering that I am really basically different from Vic Mackey, there is still a lot of me in him. I have a little bit of a jock mentality from playing sports as a kid, and that's a part of his character. I try to capture my most confident side for Vic. Then, there is an insecure side of me that I don't reveal in Vic's character. You access parts of your personality to write a character. However, it's interesting that also, as I run this show, I'm in a position of command, similarly to how Vic is with his team. This position contrasts with the one I had when I originally wrote the pilot. I was then a medium-level writer on a show. Now, I have more parallels to Vic Mackey. I can better understand him now that I am a showrunner and the boss of many people. I'd also like to think that I'm a far better husband and father than he is. On the other hand, I am not as brave as he is. He throws himself into situations that I would never have the guts to be involved in. I think it's much easier to be brave writing on the page than being brave in real life.

AMY SHERMAN-PALLADINO: The character of Lorelai in *Gilmore Girls* expresses a lot of my yapping and opinions. She is a nice vessel to use when I am angry at something and I want to get a point across. Lorelai's mother, Emily, is also incredibly fun to write for. I love the family cycle that we all get sucked into. What I'm referring to is the natural family cycle that at one moment sees everyone hugging and in the next instance, sees everyone arguing about something. I love writing about that because it is the truth in all families. Every character is fun to write for on *Gilmore Girls*.

DAVE HACKEL: I hope that both the good parts and the bad parts of me as a person are in the characters I create. However, I get asked this question a lot: "Who is John Becker? Is it you? Is it one of the other writers? Is it what Ted

Danson is really like?" I'll answer, "No, it is just as much you as it is me." They'll answer, "Me? You've just met me. How can it be me?" I then ask, "What's happened in the last day or two that has really pissed you off?" They reply with something like, "Well, I called the phone company this morning and I was kept on hold for 30 minutes without speaking to anyone. When someone finally picked up the line, I really yelled at them." So, I will answer, "Then, you are John Becker." Becker is the guy who walks into the bakery where everyone is in line with a number in their hands, and he just cuts past everyone and walks to the front of the line. All the customers get pissed and he says, "Relax I'm just getting a donut." Everyone else's response to themselves is, "What a jerk!" This is what you want to say, but polite society says not to. When you get cut off in traffic, you say to yourself, "I wish he or she hadn't done that." Becker throws half his body outside the car and screams, "Screw off!" That's what we all want to do. Becker is you, but with a bigger mouth and without a filter. So, I decided to create a character who says what I'm really thinking. An audience member once came to the rail of the set and said, "You know why I love this show? He says what I'm actually thinking." The character of John Becker is not just me, it is you.

BILL LAWRENCE: I'm sure that anybody who writes dialogue for a television show includes his or her own sense of humor for certain characters. I would say that when it came to the creation of the characters in *Scrubs,* I based them on specific, real people. The closest I ever came to taking a bunch of my own character traits and putting them into a character I created was for Michael J. Fox's character on *Spin City*. He was kind of a cocky guy who's not really all that cocky. It's just a front. I often wrote his character with myself in mind. That doesn't happen on *Scrubs* too much.

The Rewrite Process

YVETTE LEE BOWSER: Writing is rewriting. Anybody who is a good writer will tell you that. However, there are unique situations. My understanding is that the brilliant David E. Kelley, who created wonderful shows like *The Practice, Ally McBeal,* and *Boston Public,* writes scenes on a yellow pad in pen and doesn't erase or rewrite them. He is the only writer I know of who does that. Then again, this could simply be Hollywood folklore. When I write the first draft of a script, I kiddingly label it at the top of the first page "vomit draft," just in case it gets out. [Laughing] When I am in the process of writing a new script or scenes for a new show I am creating, I will label those initial pages. It is all about disclaimers until I polish it enough to call it a "first draft."

TRACY NEWMAN: I first learned the importance of rewriting at The Groundlings comedy group in Los Angeles. I was a founding member of The Groundlings, which was established in 1972. We built our own theater in 1975 and solidified The Groundlings as an innovative comedy improv group on Melrose Avenue in L.A. Some of the famous alumni include Phil Hartman, Paul Reubens, Will Farrell, Chris Kattan, Jon Lovitz, Julia Sweeney, Kathy Griffin, and the list goes on. That was where my writing partner, Jonathan Stark, and I first met. At The Groundlings, I did a lot of sketches and then rewrote them. I am glad I learned about rewriting that early in my career because rewriting is one of the most important aspects of television writing.

Overall, I think The Groundlings is a great training ground for young performers and maybe even better for writers. If somebody came to this town and wanted to get involved in television writing, I would recommend going to The Groundlings to take introductory classes. It is important to be with a group of people who have the same overall goal as you. If you look at all of the popular shows on television today, you'll find there is a Groundlings alumnus either writing or acting.

Being in The Groundlings, learning to rewrite sketches, making them funnier, and making their endings better was an invaluable lesson in writing. I learned about the beginning, middle, and end of a script. Rewriting is really the whole thing. A script can come in from one of your staff members and, for some reason, it is way off the mark. Then, you sit in a room with four or five people and you rewrite the whole thing for the rest of the day. Sometimes it takes a while for people on staff to get the voice of the show because they didn't create the characters themselves. So, rewriting is key. You want viewers to laugh because they recognize themselves or their spouse or whomever. You want audiences to relate. So, we rewrite in order to heighten many qualities in the script.

JOSS WHEDON: I find the process of rewriting extremely rewarding. It can be like solving a fascinating puzzle. In essence, it is kind of connecting the dots. The rewriting I have done on movies like *Toy Story*, *Speed*, and *X-Men* has also helped me as a TV writer, because I'm constantly involved in rewriting. When asked by a producer to rewrite a script, you are basically given a bunch of information and parameters. They want you to fix scenes by giving them meaning, humor, or life.

BARBARA HALL: The rewriting process is really important. On the other hand, there is the rewrite for me and the rewrite for everybody else. My writing process has completely changed over the years. When I started out, I wrote rigid outlines. I've gotten to the point now where I barely write an outline for a script. By the time I write the script, it is so far planned out in my head that I write very quickly. The actual sitting down and writing part of the process only takes a long weekend because I have been thinking about it for so long. However, I have that luxury as a writer because it is my show. When I was working on other people's shows, I would write an outline and stick to it. That is what I require the writers here to do.

DENNIS LEONI: Rewriting is very important. I just finished a rewrite on a script for Showtime. My partner, Jerry Offsay, gave me some notes on the first draft. When I gave it back to him, I told him I did not want any more notes. [Laughing] Jerry called me this morning and told me the script was great and that I did exactly what he expected me to do.

Jerry used to be the president of Showtime and is really the one who is responsible for putting *Resurrection Blvd.* on the air. When I came up with the idea for the newest show I'm putting together, entitled *Black and White*, I called Jerry and asked him to be my partner on it. He agreed and off we went. Hopefully, Showtime will buy this new series.

One of the important things I learned is that the key to good writing is rewriting. That is a lesson I learned from my wife, Debbie. She started her career as an assistant in the story department at Columbia, eventually became the head of drama for ABC television, and was at the network for six years. Debbie, being a development executive, is all about making a script better. Of course, everyone wants a better script. It is your job in rewriting to process it all, throw out what doesn't work, and get the script up to speed. It is vital to have an open mind. You don't have to change the script or veer from your vision if you feel strongly about it. However, you must recognize that other people can have good ideas. The smartest thing you can do is to listen to other people's ideas.

TRACY GAMBLE: I had my first experience with rewriting early in my career. After my writing partner, Richard Vaczy, and I finished writing an episode of *Newhart*, the writing staff of the show totally rewrote our script and made it good. You're thrilled to get a writing assignment, but, then, you are heartbroken to get rewritten. You think to yourself that you have failed. However, years later, you realize that you executed what you were supposed to do—create the concept for the script. It's simply that more talented people rewrote me. Anyway, it was a big learning process for me when I first entered this business.

ILENE CHAIKEN: I actually love rewriting, and I love getting notes, basically because I'm working with very smart people on *The L Word*. The scripts on this show have evolved a lot during the rewriting process. This is primarily because the feedback that I've gotten from my writing colleagues here and from the executives working at Showtime has always been valuable. Rewriting is very, very important and something I strongly believe in.

LARRY DAVID: It all depends on what you consider rewriting. To me, a rewrite is working on a script that I did not write the first draft of or, in some cases, it's after getting extensive notes from a studio, which happens more often with movies. On *Seinfeld,* I did a lot of rewriting of other people's material.

BILL LAWRENCE: I feel that TV writing has an age-old format in the way it operates. That is, you write a script and, first, it is read at a "table read." Then, you rehearse it. In sitcoms, you refine and change the whole thing. Then, you rewrite it, rewrite it, and rewrite it. The reality is that you take that first idea that you have worked so hard on, work on it some more, and try to make it funnier. However, the odds are that the original script would have been just as good as the one you end up with. I think that half the time, the product you finally end up with is, at best, a lateral move.

One of the cool things about single-camera shows is that there are no table reads, run-throughs, and rewrites like multi-camera shows. We work really hard before we shoot the script, outlining the story and so forth. Then, once it becomes time to shoot the show, we never, ever, change the story. If something is not working, we just make it work. This process eliminates so much work, and I don't believe in my heart that a complete rewrite, like totally throwing out stories, has any real value. It has just become an accepted part of the sitcom process. With that being said, one of the best things to do, and one of the reasons it is fun to clear time for it, is to rewrite jokes up to the last second before shooting a scene. The truth is that you never know if a joke works until an actor says it in front of an audience or in front of a camera. So, I do believe in rewriting jokes on a sitcom. You want to take the time to make sure that each and every joke works. How far people will go toward achieving that is the difference between shows that pop and get the audience's full attention and shows that simply don't pop.

BRENDA HAMPTON: We are on show number 175 for *7th Heaven*, and we have done 175 first drafts. [Laughing] There isn't a rewriting process on this show. The writer of the particular episode should come in with the best draft possible. It may get tweaked a little bit, but there is not a true rewriting process on *7th Heaven*, like there is on other shows. Sure, there has been a script or two when an actor or actress has fallen out or we had to change a scene because someone has gotten sick. But, as far as the general process goes, we always talk about the episode a lot before someone sits down to actually write it.

It's very important to outline the script beforehand. Our outlines can be anywhere from 15 to 18 pages in length. We tell the story in prose and tell every aspect of the story with some of the dialogue in it. If the outline is right, the script will absolutely be right. When the writers sit down to write it, they pretty much know what to do. We always have had wonderful first drafts here, and that's because all the writers are right-on-the-money.

To me, in a sitcom, the rewriting process is very odd. The writing staff rewrites the script every day and, on Friday, I don't think what you have is as good as what they originally had on Monday. When you first hear a good joke on Monday, it is really funny. But, by Thursday, when you have heard that joke told a dozen times, and the network and studio executives have heard it a dozen times, no one thinks it's funny anymore. If you kept it intact, you would have gotten a laugh from the audience, because they haven't heard it yet, and that is what matters the most. I am not necessarily a believer in rewriting.

The Network Reactions to Pilot Scripts

DAVE HACKEL: Some people liked the pilot script of *Becker* and some people didn't. NBC passed. ABC liked it, but felt there was no place on their schedule for a show like this. The saving grace of the situation was that Ted Danson had a development deal at CBS. The president of CBS, Les Moonves, read the pilot for *Becker* and liked it. The most important factor was that Ted Danson wanted to be in it, and since Moonves was already paying him, he said, "Let's shoot the pilot." If that moment in time didn't happen, I don't think the script for *Becker*, on its own, would have ever gotten made.

JONATHAN STARK: I think ABC liked the pilot script of *According to Jim*. Tracy [Newman] and I also heard that, at the time, they weren't sure if Jim Belushi was a TV star. We premiered the year ABC was launching the Jason Alexander show called *Bob Patterson*. The network had high hopes pinned on that show to succeed. I think we flew right underneath the radar. I may be wrong on this one, but I think they genuinely thought *According to Jim* would not last longer than six episodes. The reviews were not good. Basically, reviewers were saying, "What new ground are you breaking here?" Tracy's philosophy and mine was that we weren't trying to break any new ground. We were just writing a show that would make us laugh and that had some kind of truth to it from our own lives. That's really the long and short of it. The critics will say things like, "It's not edgy." Our reply was, "That was not what we intended it to be." The audience picked up on what the show was about. A lot of people come up to me and say, "Jim is just like my own husband." I know we have succeeded when people can laugh and relate to this show.

ILENE CHAIKEN: I handed in a second or third draft, but still an early draft, of the pilot script of *The L Word*. I remember I got the phone call from the network when I was on one of my writing retreats, because I go away to write by myself. Anyway, I got a phone call from Gary Levine, who is still the executive vice president at Showtime and one of the people I work most closely with. He said, "I think we're going to make this." Usually, when you turn in your script, you don't get any immediate indication that your movie or show is going to get made. So, that was a great first response.

LARRY DAVID: They thought the pilot script for *Seinfeld* was certainly unconventional, but not in a good way. They felt that the script did not have enough of a story going for it to keep the audience interested. When we had a meeting after the run-through, NBC was suggesting all these changes, and I'm thinking, "I gotta get out of here," when suddenly I hear this guy in a very expensive suit say, "We like it the way it is. We're going with this." I thought, "Who the hell is this guy?" I never heard anybody say anything like that before. It was Alan Horn. I had never seen him before and didn't know that he was an executive at Castle Rock. We then went ahead and shot the pilot of *Seinfeld* as scripted, which is what any writer hopes for.

When I watched the completed pilot, I wasn't crazy about it, but then when I got back to New York and went to the comedy clubs, some of the comedians said they saw it and were extremely positive. I was shocked. I thought, "Maybe this is actually good."

MARK BRAZILL: Peter Roth was very supportive of *That '70s Show* at Fox. I don't know if anybody recalls this, but six or seven years ago, Fox literally didn't have a sitcom on their slate of shows. *Married... with Children* was gone. *The Simpsons* is an animation show and didn't fit in that category. Fox did not have any half-hour comedies. Interestingly, the network didn't give us a lot of notes on the pilot script at all.

Things have changed so much in the six to seven years since then. The vertical integration of all of these companies is not going to be good for television. In fact, it has proven not to be good for television. When the network and the studio are essentially one, there is no separation of church and state. It's not good. What I think needs to change is that there have to be more independent producers who enjoy a bit more autonomy. They should let the people who create shows and have a vision do precisely that—create shows.

When Alan Ball finally had freedom and didn't have a network looking over his shoulder and "noting" the crap out of his scripts, look how successful he became. If you look at *Six Feet Under* and *American Beauty,* they represent Ball not being told what to do as a writer. However, if you look at the sitcom he did, it reflects "the powers that be" imposing themselves on someone who is brilliant. They tend to shave the edges off far too much in order to have mass audience appeal. *Six Feet Under, The Sopranos*, and *Curb Your Enthusiasm*—what is better on TV than those three shows? It is not just because they are on cable television and do not have the broadcast TV restrictions regarding language.

Anyway, going back to the pilot of *That '70s Show*, Roth at Fox was very supportive and not intrusive at all. He had some really great ideas and was a valuable person to work with.

BRENDA HAMPTON: I don't remember having any extensive notes from the network about the pilot for *7th Heaven*. Maybe there were a few minor notes here and there. Now, that doesn't mean that they loved it. It could have meant that they didn't think it was going to go anywhere, so why bother giving notes? [Laughing] Basically, they may have questioned if a family show would stay on the air. Even after the pilot was made, I still thought the network didn't expect it to do anything. The network didn't really pay much attention to it at the beginning of *7th Heaven*'s run. At the time, they were concentrating on other shows. They had other priorities. We are now in the eighth season, so we must have done something correct.

BARBARA HALL: It was a relatively normal pilot process for *Joan of Arcadia*. The network was happy with the pilot script, and they gave us some new thoughts. We got the pilot to where we wanted it to be. I always said to the network that this show is what it is, and you either want to do it or you don't. We can't dress it up, water it down, or put a hat on it. I never wavered from my specific vision for this show, and CBS never asked me to. We shot the pilot and the early reaction was widely varied. Some people loved it. Some people didn't get it. Some people thought it was strange. It was a flurry of mixed opinions. I'm not quite sure what specific factors put it over the top, but I do know that *Joan of Arcadia* tested well. The next thing you know, we were on the slate.

Shooting the Pilot

Casting

MAX MUTCHNICK: All four actors on *Will & Grace* originally said "no" to doing the show. Eric McCormack was the second person we auditioned for Will, and he backed out of contention by the end of that week. Megan Mullally originally read for the part of Grace. We had seen so many actors and actresses that when Megan came in again to read for the part of Karen, we forgot that we had already seen her. When we introduced ourselves again, she said, "We've already met." We told Megan that we didn't remember her, and she didn't like us very much after that. Then, on the morning Megan was supposed to come for her network read for Karen, she did not show up because she was not interested in the part. We had to call her and convince her to come in. Sean Hayes originally said he would come in again to read only if he could read for the part of Will. That was after he gave us a pitch-perfect read for the part of Jack. Debra Messing came in last to audition and didn't want to do the series at all. Of course, she is the perfect Grace. In the end, we were extremely blessed to get these talented actors and actresses for our show.

JOSS WHEDON: When casting *Buffy*, Sarah Michelle Gellar originally read for the part of Cordelia. We cast her, but also told her we might have another part in mind for her. Well, we couldn't find anyone to play *Buffy*. The interesting thing about *Buffy* is that she was raised to be Cordelia, and one day, she became *Buffy*. The structure of the movie version was that it sort of evolved into a rite of passage. The TV show was more about the adolescent metaphor of her power and her lack of power, the interaction of society, being a teenager, and all that good stuff. Sarah had the Cordelia character in her, but, at the same time, was completely disarming. She was beautiful, but not in an intimidating way. You could accept her as somebody who was unsure of herself. The jokes were funny and the emotional scenes were emotional. Sarah Michelle Gellar turned out to be a better actress than I thought she was when I cast her.

MARK BRAZILL: Bonnie and Terry Turner and I had the mindset that *That '70s Show* was going to be like a little independent film. That was the approach I was always comfortable with, anyway. I never wanted a big spotlight shining on it. Our thought was that if we could just go in quietly and let it grow, we stood a better chance of succeeding than a show that has a lot of glitz.

There have been many stories told about the casting of this show. Topher Grace was a friend of Lindsey Turner at boarding school. He tried to get a job as a PA on another show and got turned down. Bonnie and Terry said, "You have to see this guy because he is very unaffected and organic." He came in, read, and I cast him right away. Mila Kunis lied about her age. We didn't want very young kids and aimed for kids 16 years of age or up. We didn't want to work around convoluted schedules with tutors and schooling. Mila came in, read, and Bonnie asked her how old she was. She replied, "I am going to be 18." Yeah, in about four years! She was only 14 at the time. Once she got the part and we found out her real age, we didn't care because she was such a good actress and great for the part. So, we just dealt with it. Ashton Kutcher came in late, at 5:30 in the afternoon, to audition. He had been offered the part of Bo Derek's son in *Wind on Water* and NBC was trying to close the deal with him. I sensed that Ashton was the guy to play this part. Bonnie Turner and Marcy Carsey thought he had the handsome looks of a drama guy. Ashton said, "No, I am funny!" We made the deal with Ashton right there, and it has obviously turned out to be amazing. Ashton has the looks of a male model, but is comedic like Chris Farley. He's really nice and tremendously funny. Ashton works very hard and deserves everything he has. Laura Prepon, who plays Donna Pinciotti, was first presented to us from a videotape that was sent to us from New Jersey. I felt she had "the girl next door" look—if "the girl next door" was Lauren Bacall at age 17. Donna had a really great voice and a wonderful way about her. Danny Masterson, who plays Steven Hyde, and Wilmer Valderrama, who plays Fez, were "it" right away. Nobody was even close to their auditions.

BARBARA HALL: Joe Mantegna was the first person to be cast on *Joan of Arcadia*. He came across the script and considered it at a time when it didn't look like it was going to get ordered. So, Joe read it and wanted to be in it. Mary Steenburgen came along then and wanted to be on board. We cast everyone else through the regular casting process and found out who was the part. What I do credit myself for with regard to casting is that I do like to take my time with it. I think it is the part of the process that needs the most time. I am someone who would walk away from a commitment to do a show if I didn't find the right casting. I know that this is who I have to write for, conceivably, for the next 10 years. I have to be really excited about that aspect of it, and I really have to feel that the actor truly embodies the part. Fortunately, that has always been the case. A person walks in and they are the role. That is certainly true of Amber Tamblyn and everyone else.

J.J. ABRAMS: For the lead part of Sydney in *Alias,* I cast Jennifer Garner, who I had previously cast in *Felicity*. The network was open to Jennifer, so she did the audition and rose to the occasion. Jennifer was spectacular in the auditions. One thing about Jennifer is that people think she just arrived to this part and she is some overnight sensation. That simply is not true. She has been around for years, playing smaller roles and really honing her craft as an actress. The lead part of *Alias* is very physically and mentally demanding. Jennifer has to keep up with a major physical training regimen. For some of the action sequences we shoot, Jennifer has to do them 10 times in a row. It is very hard work. She is spectacular to work with every day. I also got to cast other actors who I always wanted to work with. The casting process for this show was a great experience for me.

TRACY GAMBLE: There were two other Johns who were highly considered initially for *8 Simple Rules*. I am referring to John Larroquette and John Goodman. What was funny is that we were all sitting in Tom Shadyac's office—Tom, Michael Bostick, Flody Suarez, and myself—and we all said, "I like John, I like John, I like John." Then, we would all say, "Wait a minute, which John are you talking about?" Collectively we all wanted John Ritter in the lead role. I think John was a wonderful actor with so much range.

AMY SHERMAN-PALLADINO: The two main characters that were key to cast in *Gilmore Girls* were the mother and daughter. I always sort of knew that if we didn't find the right actress for the mother, Lorelai, the show was not going to happen. Even if you found a great Rory, it still wouldn't have happened.

Rory's character was hard to cast because when you cast teenage girls who have worked before or have done Twinkie commercials since they were six, there often is a sophistication about them that Rory couldn't have. She needed to be very smart and mature in certain ways and extremely naïve when it came to things like boys. We had many, many lovely young actresses who came in and were acting innocent, but they really didn't have the innocence. I was looking for that fresh face that hadn't been spoiled yet by publicists, managers, and appearing on *Regis & Kelly*. [Laughing] We searched everywhere and we wound up in New York. This kid named Alexis Bledel came in, and she was tired, had the flu, and was completely annoyed to be there. Alexis had never done any acting, just modeling, to put herself through college at New York University, which she was attending. She just seemed to hate us and we loved that she hated us. [Laughing] She had the same quality of innocence that Rory had. Whether Alexis was able to keep up with the grueling schedule of production that we anticipated was yet to be seen. We did know that she had the goods to play Rory. She also has a face that just lights up on camera. Alexis Bledel is going to be a big, big star. There will be no talking to her very soon. She'll become JLo in another year. [Laughing] Right now, everything you see on screen is exactly what she is. She is very shy and very bright. So, Rory was the first part that we cast.

Casting the role of Lorelai was a lot more difficult. We needed an actress who was not only good at comedy, but good at drama as well. She needed to talk a mile a minute, because the speed and the rhythm is so important on this show. Without exaggerating, that is a true skill. She had to be attractive and she also had to be strong. To me, those qualities combined are the hardest to find in an actress, and we just couldn't find it. Keep in mind that this show was slated for The WB, and The WB has a reputation of being a little kids' network. So, when you go after big stars, it's a tough sell. If *24* was being aired on The WB at that time, it would not be starring Kiefer Sutherland. It would have been starring some kid out of *American Pie*. Kiefer would not have signed on to a WB show. So, for us, it was tricky because if you went after a big-name actress, you either couldn't get the person interested or her price was too high for The WB network. We really needed to find a 32-year-old woman who was a "break-out" star, who hadn't been discovered yet.

The fact that we found Lauren Graham to play Lorelai Gilmore is amazing. Lauren was an actress who had been around, and every year she had been in a new series that, unfortunately, wound up failing. Thank God! She's a name that people in the business knew and were rooting for, but the public didn't know her yet. She was the last person we read because she was on vacation during the auditions. I actually didn't want her to read because she was still in first-place consideration for another show for NBC, and they were on the fence about whether they were going to pick it up or not. So, technically she wasn't even available. I didn't want to fall in love with Lauren for the part and have the show gear up for her in the role, only to find out that she wasn't available. However, when it came down to it, we didn't have anyone else who I thought would be right for the role. Lauren came in and I knew right away she was Lorelai. Then, when we shot the pilot with her in the role and the show got picked up, we didn't firmly have her yet. We had to wait to find out if the other show was going to get picked up or not. In the end, that other show didn't go and we were off and running with Lauren.

DAVE HACKEL: When I originally wrote the pilot for *Becker*, I had no idea who would play the part of John Becker. I may have thought it was going to have to be an actor with a tough image. In fact, when Ted Danson was suggested to me, I knew he was a great actor, but I didn't think he was John Becker. Someone here at Paramount sent him the script, but Ted wasn't interested in doing another half-hour comedy. So, his wife, Mary Steenburgen, read the script first and told Ted, "You've got to read this!" Thank God she did, because Ted read it and loved it. One day, I got a call. My assistant said, "Ted Danson is on the phone." Danson said, "I really like the script and I am betting you don't think

I'm right for the part. Frankly, I don't know if I'm right for it either, but I would love to talk to you about the script." So, Ted and I got together at his house and we talked for four or five hours straight. We spoke about what the show could be and what it couldn't be and what it should be and what it shouldn't be and what makes this guy John Becker really tick. I had a lot of thoughts and answers, and Ted jumped in with a lot with his own creative thoughts. We had a really interesting discussion. At the end of the meeting, Ted said, "I still don't know if I'm actually right for this role, so why don't we put a reading together? We'll sit around a table and I'll act out what I think this guy should be, and at the end of it, if you don't like it and I don't like it, we shake hands and walk away." I said, "Fair enough." So, Paramount got some actors together and we all sat around the table and read aloud. The reading was so much fun and Ted Danson was so good that, at the end of the reading, we looked at each other and said, "Let's do this!"

What we learned from that experience is exactly what James Burrows said to me. "First of all, Ted Danson is a great actor," Jim pointed out. "He doesn't get enough credit because he makes what he does look so easy. That's simply because he's so good at it. If you do this project with Ted, you'll be able to go further in the direction you want to go than if you do it with a known hard-ass. The public loves Ted Danson. So, no matter what he says or no matter how horrible he is to someone on-screen, there is this underlying safety net of likeability. People will say, 'Hey, that's just our Ted.'"

As I said, my first reaction was to go with someone who was mean—someone who was, in fact, a hard-ass. After seeing Ted in the role, that all changed for me. He shaped this character in a much more interesting way. "John Becker" has turned into this lonely, socially inept person who you kind of feel for. That's the dimension that a great actor like Ted Danson can add to a character.

JOSH SCHWARTZ: I'm sure that with everyone you speak to in this business, the general consensus is that casting is key to the success of any show. For instance, I feel that with the *Brookfield* pilot I wrote, I was one wrong actor away from getting the show from pilot status to an actual series. With *The O.C.,* we knew from early on that Peter Gallagher was interested in playing the part of Sandy Cohen. That was a big plus for us and made the show seem very, very real. Peter was the first guy that we cast.

Mischa Barton had been on our radar to play Marissa Cooper because she had just successfully done an episode of *The Fast Lane,* which was McG's show prior to this one. We have been a huge fan of hers since the film *Lawn Dogs,* which she starred in with Sam Rockwell. Mischa had that kind of star quality to play Marissa. You also needed to know that she wouldn't be like any girl that

Ryan had grown up with in Chino. She reflected a sophistication and beauty so vastly different from anything he had ever seen in his life.

Casting the role of Marissa Cooper was the easy part, but trying to find someone to play the part of Ryan was truly the hard part. We had it in our thinking to cast some sort of brooding Matt Dillon type. Many of the actors who came in were certainly good-looking enough to meet the requirements of the genre of the character, but they didn't reflect the intelligence or soulfulness that was essential for this main character. Then, Ben McKenzie came in very late in the process. He was supposed to be the sixth lead on a UPN show but didn't get it. Ben read for us and looked very unassuming at the time, wearing an oversized jacket. He didn't even talk to us. Ben sat down, did the material, and left. Although casting Ben would have been a different direction for us, we knew deep down that we had found our guy. He was so smart and soulful, and you had the feeling he sort of lived life to the fullest.

The part of Seth Cohen was also very tricky to cast because the network was very scared about having a "geeky" type character on the show. They wanted Luke Perry and Jason Priestley types. That was something I never wanted to do. So, it was a balancing act trying to come up with a character who wasn't that, but, at the same time, had something the network could embrace. Adam Brody had come in once before to read for the part of Seth and completely improvised his entire audition. He didn't do a single line that was scripted. At first, I thought, "Who the hell is this guy? Screw him, I never want to see him again." Then, we couldn't find anyone. We decided to bring Adam back again, and he nailed the part. Adam was able to walk the line that could reflect that he wasn't necessarily accepted by his peers. I always imagined the character of Seth would be fine when he went to college or if he grew up in Greenwich Village instead of Newport Beach. He definitely would have been one of the cool kids in a New York City high school. Unfortunately, he was living in a place where his type of independent thinking would not have been accepted. He didn't listen to music on KROQ. He actually read books, which is a highly controversial thing to do. [Laughing] As we developed the character, we made it that Seth does not truly want to be accepted, just as the Newport Beach kids don't want to accept him. That allowed us to create a different kind of "geek." Adam is great in the role.

Kelly Rowan, who plays Kirsten Cohen, was also very difficult to cast. We didn't want the character to come off as a bitch because the way the pilot was structured, it could have come off that way. Kelly came in with real warmth and an earthy quality, and we knew we could go in a lot of directions with her.

SHAWN RYAN: I had heard good things about Michael Chiklis—like he was an actor's actor and he was great to work with. What I really knew him from was the fact that his wife, Michelle, and my wife, Cathy, had been friends in Miami. So, there were a couple of times in California where we ran into them socially, like at the mall. I didn't know Michael at all, but Cathy and Michelle would say, "Hi." I would be standing a step behind Cathy, while Michael would be standing a step behind Michelle. We would just sort of nod at each other as our wives chatted.

When it came time to cast *The Shield*, our casting director said, "We got a call from Michael Chiklis' agent, and Michael would like to audition for this role." There were a couple of things that were unusual about that. Number one, off the top of our heads, from what we had seen of Michael, we didn't think he was good for this part. Secondly, this show was going to be on FX, and the station was nothing at the time. A lot of agents were dissing it and saying it was basic cable and not very important. There were a lot of actors who said, "I love the script, but I will not read for the role. However, if you want to offer me the part, I'll take it." So, Michael, who had starred in two TV shows of his own, *The Commish* and *Daddio*, said he would come in to read. I said, "I don't think he is right for the role, but if he is actually going to come in to read for the part, who am I to say no? The director, Clark Johnson, and I agreed to bring Michael in. He came in and completely knocked our socks off in the audition. It was one of those times where you think you know a particular character that you have written and then an actor comes in and shows you that character in a new and interesting way. When Michael left the room, Clark said, "He seems like a pit bull with a badge."

Michael came in early in the casting process and we wound up seeing a lot more people, but we never really could get him out of our heads. I think that we initially looked for excuses to not go with Michael. In the end, his strong performance always brought us back to him. Finally, we had sort of lived with it enough to realize that we were comfortable with him as Vic Mackey. Also, we figured as audiences lived with it, they would see him as Vic Mackey and not The Commish.

Selecting a Director

BILL LAWRENCE: For me, a director of a single-camera show has to have a combination of things. The director should be able to bring something visual to it. He or she may have a cool style that I am attracted to. However, the most important thing is that the director understands the tone and the pace of the show and the humor beforehand. Then, they can step in and do the show the way it's supposed to be done, rather than make it their own.

What is tough about hiring directors in the single-camera genre is that you can't really hire movie directors. The motion picture is a director's medium, where the director can take the script and do with it what he or she essentially wants. Television is a writer's medium. In sitcoms, the directors are just making sure that they are getting all the material down and filmed. In the single-camera genre, you do not want directors to come in and say, "Okay, I'm now going to make my own little movie." The director is supposed to come here and do exactly what you want. To me, the most important thing is that I should not have to tell them about the show. I want the director to already comprehend the tone, the pace, and the jokes of the show before they walk into work.

JONATHAN STARK: There are certain directors that studios like to use. They have deals with them and also feel more comfortable with them. A studio may give you a list of the directors you can choose from. It's not like you can go around Hollywood and choose anyone you want.

The director we chose to shoot the pilot for *According to Jim* was Andy Cadiff. He had a really great track record of getting pilots on the air. He went on to direct six episodes, and he got along great with Jim Belushi.

When selecting a director, you want a director who has a sense of humor. We're not on the stage every minute and are usually upstairs in the writers' room. So, you want a director down there who says, "Oh yeah, this is funny and we'll show it to the writing team on the run-through." The cast and the director can come up with some funny ideas we haven't thought of. We are open to any ideas from anyone as long as they are funny. We have even taken suggestions from the camera guys. Anything that makes me laugh, I will put in the show.

MAX MUTCHNICK: I'm not sure if *Will & Grace* would have happened if director James Burrows did not sign on to do it. It was an edgy script at the time, but, today, it is no big deal at all. However, back then, it was something that a network would be scared about. Jimmy Burrows, who directed every great television show that NBC has seen over the last 20 years, read the pilot script and said, "I want to make it." I would say that Jimmy Burrows signing on was the stamp of approval for NBC to go ahead with making the show. It made a big difference, and he brought enormous contributions to this show. Jimmy Burrows basically said to NBC, "Back off. It's good. Don't worry about it." Having Burrows on the soundstage during the week we shot the pilot for *Will & Grace* was incredible. He told NBC that there were no notes to be given by the network, and that we were shooting the episode as scripted. That was amazing. When do you write a pilot and shoot it without getting any network notes? Burrows felt that a lot of notes from the network would really weaken the material, and he kept everyone away from us. As a result, we wrote a very clear, clean, strong pilot. That's what you need in order to make a series work. It proved to us that without a doubt, a strong director is crucial.

BRENDA HAMPTON: I always want to work with a director who knows and understands television. I like men and women directors who've been around television for a long time and know what television directing is all about. Like the writing, the directing is limited to time and budgets. You need to have a director who truly comprehends that. You must hire a director who understands that he or she doesn't have three days to get a particular scene shot. The director only has an hour and a half. You have to not only understand the creative side of directing television, but the business side as well.

I have someone who started his directing career with *7th Heaven*, Joel Feigenbaum. Joel is one of my favorites and did his first show with us during the first season and has continued to direct. I also have director Harry Harris, who has been around since *The Waltons*. I love Harry. He is great. I really enjoy working with both of them and with certain others as well.

Overall, the director has to obtain the proper coverage, because in the end, it's all about editing and cutting the show correctly. That's the bottom line.

JOSH SCHWARTZ: The idea for *The O.C.* was formed with McG and for him to direct it. Shortly before we were going into production, he had some unexpected issues involving scenes in the *Charlie's Angels* movie he directed and had to go and reshoot them. McG had to, unfortunately, drop out of our project. That was a week when the sky was falling. The network was furious and the studio was furious. I think we had enough momentum that it would have been hard to completely derail the show. However, we still had no director. That was when Doug Liman, who skillfully directed *Swingers* (starring Jon Favreau and Vince Vaughn) and *The Bourne Identity* (starring Matt Damon), stepped in to direct. It was immensely helpful. Having those two guys, McG and Doug Liman, involved made a huge difference. It put us on the studio's and network's radar much more than if the show had just myself involved.

LARRY DAVID: I look for someone who I can tell what to do and not have them get too upset about it. [Laughing] Seriously, you want to work with someone you like, who has a good sense of humor, and has good ideas. I'm much more dependent on the director in *Curb Your Enthusiasm* because I'm acting. So, it's more collaborative in that sense.

BARBARA HALL: I look at a visual style, performances, and humor. Our show, *Joan of Arcadia,* is really tricky because it walks the line between being dramatic and being funny. I have to see evidence that people have a sense of irony. My thinking is that style can never take the place of substance. I am someone who loves some cinematic techniques that are no longer used. It could be utilizing a lock-down shot or an elegant dolly move instead of using a steadicam. Also, I often use a director I already know. Jim Hayman, who is the director/producer of our show, has worked with me before. So, I knew that Jim would be great with this project.

The selection of a director also depends on the project itself. Marrying the director to the project is key. There are a lot of excellent directors on *Joan of Arcadia* who directed for *Judging Amy.* Then, we have discovered new directors.

AMY SHERMAN-PALLADINO: Selecting an outside director is sometimes easy and sometimes tough. As a writer, you can only hope that the director can really bring up your material and make it better than it already is.

Sometimes there is a feeling of combativeness between writers and directors that I feel is very harmful to the process. I've come to understand why that is. A part of me feels it's because of the unions, but I don't exactly understand why we are still so at odds, since we are actually working for the same goal. If the show looks good and it's well received, then everyone benefits. If the show is sloppy and doesn't have a focus, vision, or a look, then everyone looks bad. So, my philosophy is for all of us to just work together in peace.

DENNIS LEONI: When selecting a director, you want somebody who is exciting visually. You also want somebody who moves the story along and has the talent of getting the best performances possible out of the actors and actresses. It's key to have all those qualities in a director. There are also a lot of terrific directors out there, but they might not be right for your show. Some directors are better with talent while others are better with the camera. Sometimes you have to make a tradeoff.

Jesus Trevino directed the pilot for *Resurrection Blvd.* Not to get preoccupied with anything to do with race or nationality, but Jesus had that natural sensibility for the material because he is a Mexican-American who lived in East Los Angeles since he was five years old. I have never lived in East Los Angeles, so I wanted a director to bring that authenticity to the show. Jesus not only did that, but he is known as a terrific shooter who works on his visuals really well.

The reason I gravitated toward series television is because, as a writer/ executive producer, I have the final word. I knew that I was going to get the performances I wanted because I got to actually make the casting choices. That was crucial in my opinion. Jesus did have a say in the casting, as did the studio and the network. However, I fought for all the people I wanted to cast in the show. Very luckily, I got pretty much everyone I wanted to cast. So, I knew going into shooting the pilot that I would get good performances.

Jesus had some good ideas about the visuals, as well as recommending some other Latino creators who could give us authentic Latin music. He suggested Joseph Julian Gonzalez, who was our composer and who did a tremendous job on the show. He suggested editor Juan Garza, who turned out to be a terrific editor, and whom I'm very fond of to this day. Hopefully, we'll work together again soon. I worked with a lot of great people on *Resurrection Blvd.* I really wanted to create a familiar atmosphere on the set, and if I didn't succeed in anything else, I think I did succeed in that.

ILENE CHAIKEN: During the first season of *The L Word,* I was looking for film-makers. We initially made 13 new episodes and I did not work with any so-called "TV directors." What I mean is that, by my definition, "TV directors" are people who simply direct episodes of television, going from episode to episode, and that is what they do. Every director I worked with on *The L Word* was a filmmaker first. I worked with filmmakers whose work I liked and who were sympathetic to the tones and issues of the show. I was looking for style and point-of-view. I was really interested in the idea that each filmmaker could come and bring his or her own style and point of view to the show. I don't think that we asked anyone to conform to a style that we had set. I feel that we were able to do that because the characters are really defined and remain consistent to who they are. If I look at the 13 episodes we made, they are very different from one another, even though they all feel like the same show. I am going to direct an episode for the first time in this upcoming season.

SHAWN RYAN: For the unique look of *The Shield*, I have to give all credit initially to director Clark Johnson. When the whole pilot experience started for me, I was really overwhelmed. At that point in my career, I had worked as a television writer steadily for only four years. I really had not mastered the pro-fession. I knew there was a lot of stuff I didn't know, and visual style was one of them. So, essentially, I hired Clark Johnson, who was the best director I knew. I sat down with him and said, "Here is how I want the show to feel." We agreed on my views and we talked back and forth about a lot of things. I then stayed out of his way and trusted his visual style. When I got the dailies from the first day of shooting the pilot, I had no idea how the show would look. Clark portrayed the story the way I visually wanted it to be portrayed. Clark was really the one who set the template in terms of visual style for *The Shield* with his direction. Now, I spend a lot of time in the editing room to make sure this look stays consistent.

YVETTE LEE BOWSER: It's great when you have a longstanding relationship with a director. You eventually develop a shorthand with him or her, and it can help the process move a lot more quickly and smoothly. I'm a very collaborative person, but I always try to be very clear with what I want to achieve. When you don't know what you want to ultimately achieve with your show, then you usually run into trouble, because you give that director an opening to run free. I'm not suggesting that writers should become dictators, but it is imperative for you as a show creator to have a clear vision. Directors respect that.

MARK BRAZILL: I think you have to first ask yourself if you can get along with the person you're considering to direct. You must have a solid rapport with the director, because you are going to spend a lot of time together. It's really important if you can communicate well with that person. In film, the director is in control and the writer has a lot less input. In television, the writer/creator/executive producer has a lot of input into what finally happens. As far as television directors are concerned, I ask myself, "Can I communicate with him or her? Can I get across to him or her what I need?" That is what the director, David Trainer, represents to me. He and I are on the same page much of the time. David has been great.

TOM FONTANA: We had a lot of great and seemingly unusual choices for directors on *Oz*. My philosophy is that when you are planning a TV season, whether it's twenty-two episodes or eight episodes, you want writers and directors who understand the show you are making and who then teach you something about the show you didn't already know.

In my mind, you want to have four kinds of directors coming into a series. First, you want to have directors you can rely on. These directors have done the show, know the actors, know the rhythm, and can keep it on budget. Second, you want a group of people, like actors, who can also direct and bring a different kind of awareness to directing. I have had actors and actresses direct episodes of *Oz*, including Steve Buscemi, Matt Dillon, Kathy Bates, and Chazz Palminteri. They're good because what happens in a series is that everyone gets comfortable. The actors get comfortable with each other and with their characters. What you do when you bring in an actor who directs is that they know all the tricks. So, you have Kathy Bates saying to an actor, "Hey pal, I know what you are trying to do here and I'm not buying it!" What happens is that the actors get rejuvenated in their parts. Third, I like to hire feature-film directors. You say this is the haiku that we try to do every week, but within that you can make up your own haiku. As long as it hits a certain number of beats, you can create anything you want. The fourth and final group, which is the most fun, is the people who have directed a short film or a student film. What you get from them is the hunger, which I think is a huge part of creative energy. I think hunger is the best thing. You give me somebody who's hungry and I will give him or her as much room as they want, as long as they give me themselves. I love hiring directors who have never directed for television because you get a "balls out" result. In a way, let's consider somebody for the moment who's directed five episodes of *ER* and six episodes of *The West Wing.* That person may be a bit too formulaic. He or she may have been around too long and might have slowed down. I don't want that. I want them to shoot from the moon. With *Oz,* if you can get up there, shoot from there.

Directing Yourself

AMY SHERMAN-PALLADINO: Directing is so different from writing. Writing is very solitary and directing is hanging out and interacting with a bunch of cool people. Don't get me wrong, they're both a lot of hard work. When you are alone in your room writing, you are saying things to yourself like, "I suck. I have no talent." But when you are directing, you are with a whole crew who you can turn to for an idea if you are stuck or experiencing a problem. Plus, crews are a lot of fun. You are up early drinking a lot of coffee and eating junk food. It's a very tedious process to get it from paper to film, but when it gets there, it's very gratifying.

I think if you direct it personally, instead of someone else directing your written material, you can go from 70% of the way you wanted the show to look to 90%. Is it ever going to be 100% of what I intended? No. However, I know with me directing the episode that it'll be as close to the mark as it ever will be. There are other factors that come into play when you're trying to get your vision to the screen. If your actress broke up with her boyfriend the night before and she has to do a funny scene that day, it might not turn out as funny as you may have liked. As a director, you have to get it close enough to where you want it to be, under any given circumstances.

When somebody else is directing your writing, it can be wonderful and sometimes it can be off. As a writer, you can only hope that the director can really bring up your material and make it better than it already is. Also, sometimes there's a feeling of combativeness between writers and directors that I feel is very harmful to the process.

If you are a writer and you want to protect your writing, you absolutely have to direct it yourself. No one else is going to protect the written word and concept for you. If you're not going to direct your writing, then you can't really complain that it didn't come out completely the way you envisioned it to. It essentially becomes someone else interpreting your material with their own eyes. This is the very reason why I started directing. I decided to direct because I genuinely wanted to see if it's possible to get something that I had envisioned written on paper exactly the same way on film.

ALAN BALL: When it came to *Six Feet Under,* I had never run an hour-long show. In fact, I had never worked on an hour-long show. The only experience I had with a single-camera shoot was when I was on the set of the movie I had written, *American Beauty.* During the year it was in production, I just sort of observed. HBO asked me, "Who do you want to direct the pilot for *Six Feet Under?*" I replied, "I do." I knew that one of my long-range goals was to write and direct my own work, whether it be feature films or TV. I thought HBO would say, "That's really funny, but seriously, here is the list of directors you can choose from." To my pleasant surprise, they agreed to let me direct it. Much later, I found out that they were very nervous about me directing.

It was a really good experience for me. Directing the pilot for *Six Feet Under* was exhilarating and terrifying at the same time. I have never been to film school and I know very little about lenses and filters and that sort of stuff. However, I was working with some really talented people. I worked with a terrific producer, Alan Poul, and an excellent director of photography, Alan Caso. I spent a lot of time prepping with Alan Caso. I would say things like, "I want this shot to feel sort of intrusive," or I would say, "When we are with this character, I want him to look really vulnerable." He was excellent at achieving that. I knew I couldn't do it all by myself, so I depended on the talented people I hired. Ultimately, I think that is the best approach to running a show or directing a movie. Basically, you surround yourself with the best people you can and get out of their way. Unless, of course, you see they are going in a direction that you know is wrong. I'm not one of those people who feels like every decision has to be mine and every moment has to be something that I came up with. I think that's sheer egomania, and I also just don't want to work that hard. I'm smart enough to realize that other people are going to have other good ideas and some of those ideas are going to be better than the ones that I have. I think it's important to use the best ideas and the best moments, because in the end, the final work is the most important thing, and it always has to be.

BILL LAWRENCE: I have directed episodes of *Scrubs* myself, and it can be really tedious. You're sitting around and waiting a lot of the time. On the other hand, what's really fun is to rehearse the scenes and work on the jokes with the actors. In single-camera technique, for three characters to have a conversation, you have to shoot each one of them talking to the other person and take different shots for coverage, et cetera. It can take hours just to shoot one scene. That, to me, is painstaking. On the other hand, telling people how to say the jokes to make them pop is fun. The best reason for me to direct single-camera, as opposed to multi-camera in a sitcom, is that it's surprisingly easy to distance yourself from the crew. You keep writing and they keep working. It's a machine in constant motion. Directing for me is a great way to remind myself how hard everyone works and how the process proceeds once we hand them the script.

LARRY DAVID: I've only directed one movie and I wasn't exactly Ernst Lubitsch back there. I'm sure the crew was constantly rolling their eyes at some of the idiotic questions I was asking. Mind you now, I've never even owned a camera. If you asked me to take a picture with your camera, I wouldn't have the foggiest idea of what to do. I suppose I've never been interested in keeping a pictorial record of my life.

Production of the Pilot

YVETTE LEE BOWSER: The production for the pilot of *Living Single* went very smoothly. I trusted my instincts and worked with a director who, at the time, seemed like the appropriate person for the series primarily because he fully respected my vision. There wasn't a power struggle between us. So, it was a great experience for me, but it could easily have gone differently. There could have been a ton of people coming in and telling me what the show should be. I did get a lot of notes along the way, and some of those notes were confusing. I remember that one network executive kept saying, "This is really good, but it needs to be 10% funnier." Well, I work with words, not numbers. So, I had no idea what he meant by that. To this day, I don't know what that means, but I clearly know what I'm doing in terms of writing half-hour television. Today, if a network executive said, "Make it 10% funnier," I would respond, "Okay, next note please." I need someone to tell me where they feel it's not humorous and I will try to make it funnier. Usually, writers and executives have a strange relationship, but it's nothing personal. I have luckily and thankfully had the sincere pleasure of working with some of the brighter and more creative executives over the years.

MARK BRAZILL: I felt the production of the pilot for *That '70s Show* went well. I wasn't sure if it would work or if the network would like it or if the show would even get on the fall schedule. However, I liked the way the project turned out and I liked the characters. Initially, it was probably broader than it should have been, but the show eventually became more refined through the seasons that followed. In one way, it looked familiar, and in another, it looked like nothing I had ever seen.

Terry Hughes directed the pilot. Terry had been the director on *3rd Rock from the Sun*. After him, we got director David Trainer, who previously directed on the sitcom *Cybill*. During my first four seasons, he was an important partner to me. He was so good at corralling the young cast members. Aside from Danny Masterson and Mila Kunis, the rest of the kids had never been on a set before. Trainer was tremendous at running our soundstage.

I felt that we really captured that particular decade in the pilot episode. During the production of the pilot, we tried to do stuff in the style of what was available in the 1970s. When Eric and his friends got high in the pilot, we just physically moved the wall to create the effect. Two grips grabbed the corner of the wall and moved it up and down. We didn't use CGI and we tried to do everything according to the techniques that were available production-wise in era of the '70s. Everybody became very anal about the time period. The crew really cared a lot about the costumes and the sets being truly authentic to the decade of the '70s. We shot the opening credit sequence for the show in the car in the middle of the night with a tow truck attached to the car. It was a unique bonding experience, spending those couple of weeks together, and I think everyone realized how much fun we could have doing this show. It felt really great and I knew this was something I could do every week.

BARBARA HALL: Both of my shows, *Judging Amy* and *Joan of Arcadia,* were shot as presentations and not full-length pilots. The basic reason was because both shows were ordered so late in the game that we could only do a presentation. I am the person who is known for doing presentations because I like that format now. The production of *Joan of Arcadia* went fine. I genuinely liked the pilot. When it was ordered, we had to go back and make the full-length pilot. We didn't actually re-make it, we just added to it. We shot the presentation like a film. It was 30 minutes in length, but it was exactly like making a full-length show.

DENNIS LEONI: Early on during the pilot, I had to sort of fight with Showtime for a level of independence, because they wanted me to have a showrunner come in and work with me from the very beginning of *Resurrection Blvd.* All networks want you to have a showrunner to oversee the daily operation of a show. On *McKenna*, the show I was writing for before creating *Resurrection Blvd.*, I was a co-producer, but I never ran a show before. When I was putting the deal together with Showtime, I had to convince them every step of the way to give me the freedom to follow my own specific vision. Finally, I agreed with Showtime to meet with a few showrunners. However, I was always leery about a showrunner being involved, because *Resurrection Blvd.* is very culturally specific, and I did not want somebody to come in and usurp my vision.

I eventually talked Showtime into letting me write the pilot script alone. I wrote the script, they read it and really liked it. Then, Showtime wanted to bring in an executive producer. I asked them not to do it, and I explained that most Latino shows fail because they are done by people who don't really know the culture. For once, I wanted to be allowed to do a show that I knew a lot about. I eventually talked them into letting me shoot the pilot without a showrunner. Showtime loved the way the pilot turned out and it tested through the roof. We tested it as a feature and it did absolutely great! However, when it came time to do the actual series, Showtime told me I had to have a partner because I had never run a show before. They felt I did not have the experience. For instance, I never ran a writers' room before. I never oversaw the editing, the directing, or the background music of a show. I agreed to having a showrunner present, but I recommended a friend of mine named Bob Eisele. Bob Eisele came on *Resurrection Blvd.* as my partner and he helped me every step of the way. He is a wonderful, talented guy, and it worked out tremendously.

ILENE CHAIKEN: The production for the pilot of *The L Word* was a great experience, intense and challenging. It was the first time I had ever produced my own work. In fact, it was more like making a film because it was a two-hour pilot. So, I tried to step back to the extent that I wanted the director, Rose Troche, to feel like she was making her own movie. At the same time, it was, in fact, my show and my script and I had a lot of proprietary interest and also, ultimately, the authoritative role. During the production of the pilot, I was constantly figuring out how the crucial balance would work. It was a balance that had to be found and was not always readily accessible. In other words, sometimes we were in conflict. But, in the end, it was the most successful realization of my work that I had ever experienced. Rose Troche directed a pilot that very explicitly reflected the story I wanted to tell and the characters I had written. The pilot was everything that I imagined it could ultimately be. It was very gratifying.

BILL LAWRENCE: Doing the pilot for *Scrubs* was next to impossible. *Spin City* was a multi-camera show, so *Scrubs* was a new experience for me, because shooting single-camera is totally different. Single-camera is like a freight train. It's not like you rehearse all week and then do it in front of an audience, which is what multi-camera is. In single-camera, you have five days to get all of this material shot. You have to worry about staying on budget. You go home to sleep after a long day of shooting and then you wake up the next day, go back, and keep shooting, shooting, shooting.

We basically spend five days a week making a small 30-minute movie, and I think the end result is visually attractive on screen. You won't find, even on an independent film, that it takes any less than two months to shoot a film that runs for an hour and a half. For us, we shoot an hour and a half film in just 15 days. You find that a big feature-film hospital movie takes at least three months to shoot. That's not even counting preproduction and postproduction. We do all of it in only three weeks. First, we do preproduction for a week prior to shooting the episode. Then, we shoot the episode. The following week, we edit it and then keep moving on. It was a real shock for me during the production of the pilot for *Scrubs* to see how quickly things move with a single-camera approach in television. TV is truly about staying on budget and not being hugely expensive. One of the appealing factors of this show is that it's one of the cheapest single-camera comedies made in this business. We shoot *Scrubs* guerilla-style in five days. Most single-camera comedies are on six-day shoots per episode, if not more.

Once the Pilot Goes to Series

Marketing the Show

DAVID KOHAN: *Will & Grace* premiered on a Monday night. During the "up-fronts" in New York [which is where the networks announce their new fall lineup each year], there was no mention that the characters Will or Jack were gay. They marketed it as, "It's just a show about best friends." Then, they put it on Monday night, which they nicknamed, "Must-SHE TV," because it was sandwiched between *Suddenly Susan, Caroline in the City*, and *Veronica's Closet*. It was a quiet night for NBC, so they thought they could ease *Will & Grace* in. The following year, our show moved to Tuesday night. However, it wasn't until the third year that it had a real high-profile image. When *Will & Grace* finally moved to the Thursday night lineup, it was never considered controversial because it already had two years under its belt. It sort of slowly became part of the network landscape. We didn't have any real controversy surrounding us because it was never "splashed" out there.

JONATHAN STARK: The marketing of our show *According to Jim* is an interesting story. In May, when networks traditionally announce the new shows, they have the "up-fronts" in New York. We got invited to go because our show was being presented. As we arrived at the event in the limousine, they told us that they had decided to name the show *The Dad*. We saw all of these yellow and black signs with Courtney Thorne-Smith and Jim Belushi kissing and over it were the words "The Dad." It was shocking. I yelled, "What!?" The reason they wanted to do that was because that year ABC-TV had a night they called "D-Day." The reason they called it that was because they had Damon Wayans, Drew Carey, and Denis Leary all on the same night. With Jim Belushi scheduled for that evening, there was no "D" in the title or his name. Therefore, by calling it *The Dad*, they got the "D" in there.

My writing partner, Tracy [Newman], and I said, "Oh, no!" I told the network that even though there are kids in the show and he's a father, it is more about the romantic and comedic relationship between a man and a woman. I was never big on writing family comedies, so I did not want it sold like that. The network then asked, "What do you want it to be called?" We thought a lot about it, but couldn't come up with anything that worked. Finally, Tracy's boyfriend came up with *According to Doyle,* which was a take-off of a name based on a card-playing rules book, *According to Hoyle.* Since we didn't have a last name, we thought it might work. Well, we didn't want to make him Irish, so we came up with *According to Jim.*

JOSH SCHWARTZ: The sheer volume of advertising and publicity and the way Fox went about building ads to promote *The O.C.* was a pleasant shock to me. The studio really got behind this show and it has been amazing. It was a real vote of confidence and totally exciting. The best line I saw was one where the top banner of some magazine read: "We are hyperspazzing over *The O.C.*" However, I wanted to make sure that we had our own identity. The *90210* comparisons are something that I have always understood: Both shows were launched in the summer. Both stories are about beautiful, young, affluent people living in Southern California. However, for me, that was never the kind of show that I wanted *The O.C.* to be. On the other hand, *90210* had a very passionate following and I figured that if our fan base developed at least half that passion, then it would be a great thing. I still want our show to continue to be unique.

LARRY DAVID: HBO will run the ads and promos by me for *Curb Your Enthusiasm.* They'll show me the "one-sheet" ads and then show me the on-air promos prior to their airing. At the beginning of *Seinfeld,* I did not have much to do with the marketing. I generally hated all the TV promos that NBC came up with. I thought they were really lame and embarrassing. They would have some idiotic voiceover reminding people, hammering them over the head, to watch the show. Often, they would give the jokes and story away in the promos and would take anything that had to do with sex out of context. All in all, I could not stand their marketing approach.

ILENE CHAIKEN: The marketing aspect of *The L Word* was a huge challenge at Showtime. I know a lot of thought, conversation, research, and exploration went into it. Ultimately, they did a really amazing job. The questions were two-fold. How do we market the show to a gay and lesbian audience? How do we broaden the market, because that is how the show will ultimately either live or die? Naturally, the show had to be speaking to the core audience.

I'm extremely happy how the marketing for the show turned out. I never had any complaints of "Oh my God, I can't believe they are doing this. I hate that poster." Showtime was very, very collaborative and respectful of me. They always consulted me and included me in their marketing decisions, even though it was clearly understood that I have already done my job and this was their job.

MARK BRAZILL: One of the things *That '70s Show* has is a built-in motif, the decade of the 1970s. It's a lot easier for a studio to market a show that has that. For instance, when Disney put out *Pocahontas*, they made Indian blankets with patterns on them. So, Fox did the same thing for our show, latching on to things like 8-Tracks, bell-bottoms, and lava lamps, which all tied into the title of our show and the decade. I really complained that first year. I felt we really had to sell the people on the show, not just the bell-bottoms. I remained steadfast that the bell-bottoms weren't what's funny about this show. I knew from the beginning that as the show went on, the faces of these characters were going to keep the audience coming back.

BARBARA HALL: When CBS put *Joan of Arcadia* in its primetime schedule on Friday nights at eight, I fully understood what they were thinking of in terms of marketing. This was an attempt to get a crossover audience, in particular, a younger one. At that point, our show was being discussed for Sunday nights at eight, and I actually did not want that slot. I felt that it was the *Touched by an Angel* slot and there might end up being a misinterpretation of the show and it might skew much older. I really liked what CBS was saying by positioning us on Friday nights at eight.

Hiring a Writing Staff

YVETTE LEE BOWSER: I hire writers who, for the most part, are funnier than I am. I hire people who have different cultural and socio-economic experiences so that there's a real dialogue in the room and genuine diversity. I think that it comes through in the episodes and the points of view expressed by the characters. That's been my approach since the beginning. Over time, you discover who on the writing staff really can and who really can't do the work. You keep hiring people and you politely let the others go.

There's also the mentoring component to what I do. It's very important for me to be a mentor to others. When I look back on my career, that's something I'm very proud of. I'm trying to find other people who started like me without the opportunities and I give them that shot. I like to nurture them and give them an opportunity. The best part is to see them go on to their own individual success. Several people that I've helped out along the way now have their own shows and some are co-executive producers on other shows. It's rewarding to see! I feel that I've done what I set out to do and then some. Most importantly, I'm not, by any means, finished with helping people. I'm glad that I've done something significant for others in addition to making a career for myself.

JOSH SCHWARTZ: Hiring a writing staff was totally new to me when I created *The O.C.* I was 26, and, because of my age, the network felt I could relate to these younger characters. However, when it came time to get serious and build the infrastructure of the show, the network wanted to find someone who could handle all of those responsibilities. That's completely understandable, because I had never been on a show before or staffed a show with writers. They wanted me to work with someone who was experienced and seasoned in order to pull that off. I got the gift of executive producer Bob DeLaurentis. Bob DeLaurentis has been a huge help and was instrumental in hiring our great writing staff. I think Bob's experience was key in helping me find the most talented writers possible. He is absolutely fantastic.

When we shot the pilot, we had some real high-profile executives involved, like McG and director Doug Liman, who are extremely talented. However, it was clear that when and if we went to series, these people had definite commitments and would not be on the team to run the show on a day-to-day basis.

JOSS WHEDON: We are out there looking for new and talented writers all the time. It took the run of *Buffy* to get a staff that I was completely confident in. The last two years were the first years that I actually didn't have to let go of a writer.

If you do have outstanding talent, it's difficult for you not to get noticed. However, there's one crucial factor with regard to getting a writing job, and that's the concept of functioning in the writers' room. I figured out that some people don't work well in the writers' room and some do. You, as a writer, have to mesh well with the producers. At one time, I didn't think that way: If someone wrote a great script, but did not mesh well with the producers, I thought, "If you put those words down, it really doesn't matter." In every single one of those cases, that person didn't last. Over the long term, we just couldn't communicate. I'm very adamant about running a friendly and non-competitive room. That doesn't mean we don't make fun of each other constantly. [Laughing]

Some shows are rooted in writing-staff competition. I just can't work that way. I loathe competition. The only sport I like is Hacky Sack because there is no winner. When people come into my employ, they will jokingly get made fun of, but I will also offer them a place of safety, where everyone is going to do their best and nobody is going to be better than anyone else. You have to hire people that you can be in a room with for a long time. I have known talented people who have made a bad impression in a room and didn't get a job, but turned out to get hired somewhere else and turned out to be solid writers and great people.

JONATHAN STARK: There weren't that many writers we knew who were available at the time we staffed *According to Jim*. Once agents get wind that there's a new series getting picked up by a network, they send piles and piles of scripts. Tracy [Newman] and I hate to read through spec scripts, so our executive producer, Suzanne Bukinik, read through them, and she made three piles of scripts marked good, bad, and maybes. I would read all of the ones in the good pile and confirm with Tracy. Then we would call the writers in for a meeting. We met writers for a couple of weeks all day long. Through that process of hiring a writing staff, we met some really talented people. Many of the writers that we had at the beginning of the show, we don't have on staff now. It's not the fact that they are not good writers. They just didn't jive with the voice of our show, but, again, that doesn't mean they aren't good writers.

ILENE CHAIKEN: I didn't know exactly what I was looking for when I was hiring a writing staff. As a writer, it is hard to let anybody else write for your characters. I looked for the best writers I could find. I asked Rose Troche, after she worked on the pilot as a director, if she would be on my writing staff. She is currently a coordinating producer on the show. I also looked for writers who had done television and could help me and walk me through the process if it got rocky. Mainly, I was looking for really smart, literate writers whose voices felt like they could coincide with mine. I also wanted them to bring something unique to the show. The most exciting thing to me about the whole process is the group writing in the writers' room. I come into the room and say something like, "These are the stories I want to tell this year." Then, everything is opened up to this small team of writers. The ideas get so much better and they go so many places that you never could have imagined on your own. It is never about one person. It is about the group process. It is about the way we react and interact with one another.

DENNIS LEONI: When your show gets picked up and it's time to hire a writing staff, the studio puts out calls to all of the agents and they send hundreds of sample scripts. Then, you get the best help you can to read all of those scripts. At the time of *Resurrection Blvd.*, the studio was reading scripts, the network was reading scripts, as were the executive producer, Bob Eisele, and myself. It was a thorough process.

There were a few types of writers I was looking for when hiring a writing staff for *Resurrection Blvd.* First, it's important to find seasoned writers who can structure a script and who have the experience. Also, since *Resurrection Blvd.* is so culturally specific, I wanted to hire writers with certain sensibilities. However, it was a double-edged sword. On one hand, what I was trying to do was show how we, as Latinos, are different from the mainstream of American culture, but, on the other hand, I wanted to show how we are the same.

BRENDA HAMPTON: When I originally started *7th Heaven,* I hired about a half dozen writers. We still have a small staff now. When I was hiring a writing staff for the first season, I took whomever the network and studio thought would be helpful, along with maybe a person or two that I already knew. Most of those writers were gone by the second season. However, I did keep people whom I enjoy working with and I trust. I must have an honest dialogue, an honest back-and-forth, with my staff about the writing of the show. I find that to be more helpful than having some writer with more hours of experience.

Sue Tenney and I write most of the episodes, and she's been here since the second season. The other writers on this show have come up through the ranks. They have all started out as production assistants and have moved up to where they are today. Chris and Jeff Olsen are producers. They both started out as assistants in the office. Jeff Olsen started out as the kitchen production assistant and worked his way up to being a story editor. Shawn Kostanian started out in the same capacity, as the kitchen production assistant, and he's a co-producer now. With the help of all of these great people, I can focus more on the writing.

Does the Talent Get Involved with the Writing?

DAVE HACKEL: Ted Danson did not get involved directly with the writing of *Becker*. He values good writing and is always appreciative of what writers do. When I tell him a story, he'll say, "Wow, that sounds great, but maybe we could even do such and such." Where Ted does get involved with the writing of the show is usually in the rehearsal process. He doesn't want to be a writer or a director or a producer. He just wants to be an actor. Since he has had so much experience in this field, whether he knows it or not, he is a writer, a director, and a producer as well as an amazing actor.

Ted will say, "This scene is really funny, but it feels like something should happen here." Most of the time, I will agree he's right. An actor that's out there in the middle of the scene might have a feel for something that should happen that a writer might not be aware of. So, we appreciate our actors' input and it can really make the writing better. My attitude is, whoever has the good idea, encourage that person and throw it in! Ted Danson is just a wonderful person. With Ted and all the other actors on this show, when they act out what you wrote, they bring you something better than what you had before. We might not have been the biggest hit on television, but I don't think anyone had more fun doing it.

BARBARA HALL: No, the cast doesn't normally get involved with the writing. It is not that we shut everybody's ideas out. Actors sometimes talk to us about what they think about our characters. Or they suggest that they really want to have a scene between their character and another particular character.

I have an open-door policy. People can come in and tell me anything they want. There is a huge level of trust on this show. I do not want anybody to feel shut out, but at the same time, I feel very strongly that there needs to be a single vision behind a show and that vision needs to be executed by a lot of people. So, while we do talk to the cast, the writers remain in charge of the writing. That is something that's really important to me.

JONATHAN STARK: After the run-through on *According to Jim*, our star, Jim Belushi, and I talk a lot about the script. He suggests things and brings in stuff from his own life. Jim is actually very helpful. I appreciate that he gives us some great suggestions, and we take it from there. Like me, Jim has a wife and kids. So, getting that first-hand experience really makes the jokes and the story much more interesting when it comes from somebody's real life. Not every story we use comes from real life, but most of the ideas do. Jim Belushi doesn't come up to the writers' room and write.

ILENE CHAIKEN: No, the cast members on *The L Word* don't get involved with the writing. However, they certainly get involved with the development of their characters and storylines. They have, on occasion, suggested ideas to me that I wound up working with. It is not that they pitched stories. It's more along the lines of them talking to me about their characters and sometimes even their wishes. One actress said to me, "Do you know what I really want next season? I want to have a tender love scene with someone." Her character just sleeps with everyone and goes from one conquest to another. I didn't pay it much attention when she said it, but when I started thinking about stories, it just stayed with me. I then realized that it is the story for her character this year. We are moving toward something that is going to look like a tender love scene.

Every once in a while, the actors and actresses will open up and tell me things, because all of us have a very easy and intimate relationship. I spend time with them, which is very productive. I feel that it is vital to have that open relationship with the people you are collaborating with. I have character meetings with every one of the cast members. Actually, I'm in the midst of that now, because we are about a month away from production and they all want to know just how to be preparing. I am sitting down with each and every one of them and saying, "Here is more or less what is going to happen with your character over the course of this season." We talk about motivation and what is going on inside. They tell me their fears if they have any. Usually, it is stuff I am already thinking about and their fears have already been addressed. However, if they have concerns from a character's point of view and I have not addressed them, I usually go back and review what I've done.

Making a Show Last

JOSH SCHWARTZ: Making a show last is basically about keeping its characters relatable and allowing the audience to understand that these characters are good people who are in many ways flawed. The characters are simply trying to make their way in a world that isn't always a good world. In light of all the reality television, which has certainly become a factor, it's been very hard to invest in characters that you love, because a lot of reality TV is actually based on being punished for liking a character. You're essentially watching those characters get punished. I think our show comes along at a time when audiences are getting sick of that.

There are television characters that audiences can get involved in and grow to love and grow with them. That is a television experience that the audience might not have been able to enjoy for a while. So, as long as we can keep the audience involved with these characters and keep them extremely relatable, then, I think, *The O.C.* can continue to move forward. I think that holds true for any show, and its ultimate success in the long run depends on it.

DAVE HACKEL: I created a show called *The Pursuit of Happiness,* which barely lasted for 13 episodes. I had a good idea and I thought we had a good pilot, but I didn't have a clear vision overall of what I wanted the show to be. If you don't have a clear vision at the get-go, then it is sort of like getting in a car, putting it in drive, and driving around aimlessly. If someone asks you where you are going, you blankly answer, "I'm just driving." Eventually, you'll run out of gas and will have had a very unsatisfying trip. If you get in a car and you know you're going to New York, you can take a whole bunch of different routes, but at least you know where your final destination is.

I was in my late thirties when a friend asked me, "Didn't you think as you got older that your life would get easier? But, it just hasn't, right? It has just gotten more and more complicated." That's very true. The older you get, the more responsibility you take on. I then felt that maybe there is a television show in that. I was thinking of the story of a man who is at the point of his life when he believes things should be easier, but they're not. That was a sort of general idea for *The Pursuit of Happiness*. I sold that pilot with the guys from Grub Street to NBC because I had been there for so many years on *Wings*. The pilot was so much fun and I felt it was great. However, the hardest episode of any show is the second one. You've already told the basis of the story and have set it all up. Now, where do you want to go? So, there I was, driving with no idea where I was going. Every week, I was trying to find my direction. In the final analysis, the reason it failed was my fault. I think I had good actors in the wrong parts. I had good writers, but I couldn't give them the proper direction. Frankly, I didn't even know where we were going. I do think we did some good work by accident. When I began doing *Becker,* I had already learned quite a bit from that failure. I knew that I needed to know where I wanted the show to go so the writers could work to their top creative capacity and the show could last. I had answers because I really thought the character of John Becker through. *The Pursuit of Happiness* consisted of some good ideas in search of a great idea that never came to fruition.

J.J. ABRAMS: I think that to keep *Alias* on the air for a long time, we have to continue to tell good stories and keep them honest. I believe that every good story that we tell will feel honest because we have learned to communicate that kind of good story in the right way. I feel that if we concentrate and focus on doing that, the audience will acknowledge our efforts and keep watching. Of course, the ultimate dream would be to continue to work with such an incredible cast and crew and keep telling stories that make me, personally, smile when I think about the path that these characters have taken. You can have a general sense of it, but you don't precisely know what you are going to do years in advance. We always throw around ideas for future show plans. For me, the point of doing this show is to tell stories that are believable and relatable. These stories just happen to exist in a world that is so hyper-real and extreme that "high stakes" and "crazy" are the norm. I think the audience will continue to find this exciting as long as we stay true to what has got us to this level of success.

AMY SHERMAN-PALLADINO: Keeping a show on the air goes back to the old saying, "Too many chefs spoil the soup." If you have too many chefs in the kitchen—too many people providing input—then it's hard to stay on the air and make a TV series last. You have to protect your ideas and your writing from those outside people with opinions. All of that can dilute the product and weaken it. David Chase does not have 20 people telling him what to do on *The Sopranos.* Bright, Kauffman, and Crane did not have 20 people telling them what to do on *Friends.* David E. Kelley does not have anyone telling him what to do because no one can get into his office. [Laughing] When you don't have a hundred people telling you what to do, it gives you a chance to do something good. I think that's a key ingredient to keeping a show around for a long time.

SHAWN RYAN: To make this show last, I think it is vital to stay true to your viewers. If an idea comes too easily to me, then it would come too easily to the viewer and it would not be surprising to anyone. So, our gameplan is to always be moving forward, and I believe an audience will come with us. Naturally, there are some ideas and places that I would like to go. However, I think it's important to even surprise yourself along the way. I'm glad I don't know exactly where I want this show to go because wherever it is, I want it to be surprising, fresh, and different. That's essential to making a TV show have staying power.

TRACY GAMBLE: I think to make a show last, you must always have a depth of material to draw from. You have to derive ideas from things that are evolving around you. I'm watching my children grow up and I realize that I have plenty of new material. The stories can be heartwarming and they can be heartbreaking. My son, Rory, a year ago was my buddy. Now, this year, he is 13 years old, full of hormones, and has an attitude. So, that is coming into the show. I know that one day he will be my buddy again. My daughter Bridget is a free spirit and I want to allow her to be that. However, it also scares me. My daughter Kerry is a jock, and she was number six in the state of California in the 400-meter dash. Kerry was also a nationally ranked junior tennis player, and we want to bring that into the mix as well. As we naturally progress, it's a pre-empty-nest syndrome. One of the kids is going to leave the house, so I see no problems with the evolution of storylines.

I would definitely like to take on more serious issues, but I realize that we do have to earn it. I'd like to explore serious issues such as well-written shows like *Roseanne* did. The show was hilarious at times and was serious at times too, just like life. Unfortunately, I think that shows generally don't last long enough to have the opportunity to tackle some serious issues. You have to be on the air for a little while to be able to do serious stuff like that. I'm eager to keep writing and producing a show that will not only make people laugh, but will also make them think and reflect on their own lives.

BRENDA HAMPTON: The key to making a show last is different for each particular show. The key to making *7th Heaven* last is meeting the audience's expectations from week to week. Having grown up on a diet of family television and having watched family television, I felt that I could relate to the medium. However, I found that as a result of my coming out of half-hour sitcom writing, the boundaries I knew to be were much tighter for a family genre show. I feel that still holds true, but I like the challenge of doing it. I'm not developing any other family-genre shows right now, only because there is interest from other people in different types of shows from me. However, I definitely enjoy writing it. We have an unusually wide fan base for this show, because it ranges from ages 5 to 95. When we first started the show, Ron Zimmerman, who was on the writing staff, felt that *7th Heaven* had the capability to go on for eight years or more. He felt we were creating a classic. At the beginning, I was certainly happy to be doing the show, but I didn't have a clue whether it would go on for that long. It's a very different kind of show to write. I don't think that doing this show is hard and I love doing it.

JOSS WHEDON: One of the keys to keeping a show on the air is to listen to your fans and respect them. I have been going into chat rooms and on websites since the first season of *Buffy*. The Internet really became a community right about the time when *Buffy* became a show. That meant that I could get unprecedented audience feedback. It's been great and developed into a valuable tool because you can feel the audience out and find out what they are responding to and what they are not responding to. I used to go on the Internet after every show, and I still frequently do, to see what the viewers think. I'll often learn something I didn't know. For example, I discovered that the audience liked a character that I never really thought about. I even learned that they liked my writing more than I ever thought they would. You say to yourself, "They love me." However, you have to remember, nobody turns on you faster than somebody who loves you. My wife, who is sitting alongside me, just said, "That's not true." [Laughing] Let me rephrase it to this: It's like somebody who loves you, but doesn't truly know you. So, you can definitely hear some horrible things about yourself on these websites. They're brutally honest for the most part. When you read that an episode of the show wasn't as good as these diehard fans hoped it would be, that's understandable and acceptable. I say to myself in that case, "Okay, it's an indication that we didn't hit our mark this week." However, it's tough when they say things like, "This episode sucked. They sold out!" They take it so personally, as if they lived with you, and it's comments like this that are very disturbing. On the other hand, there are also fans who love what I'm doing. By and large, it's a really positive force. It is like having a really big drunk friend who holds nothing back and says everything openly and honestly.

The idea when creating a show is to affect people emotionally with the writing. The show is supposed to make you hurt, inspire you, and move you to laugh and cry. It's supposed to work on an extremely gut level. As a writer, that's the only way I can work. Honest audience reactions that I can personally be a part of and benefit from have become very important to me as a creator.

BILL LAWRENCE: We have to realize that there is a whole wave of shows on the air that amount to a bunch of characters on-screen just throwing jokes around. I think writers forget that in sitcoms, it's not only about the jokes, you also have to tell a story. It's not enough to just have your characters simply throw gags and jokes around at each other. For me, what ultimately makes a show last is giving people something to care about. Yeah, you have to be funny, but you also want audiences to care about your characters.

Seinfeld loved to call itself the anti-sitcom with no hugs and no lessons. Whether the show's creators and writers wanted it to end up this way or not, people cared about those characters. It was painful when you watched George Costanza tell some chick he was an architect and you knew he was going to get busted for lying. It was painful because you actually gave a crap about him. *Friends* ultimately became a melodramatic soap opera and was successful because the audience cared whether Ross and Rachel were going to end up together.

Another important show element is distinct voices. Anytime you are watching a drama or a sitcom or working on a script, the problem arises when you can just change a character name and have anyone tell that joke. To me, that is a huge red flag. That says that no character on your show is truly defined and they are not different from each other. One of the things we like about writing *Scrubs* is that all the characters are different and very individual and we can't just give anyone the same joke.

LARRY DAVID: Good reviews, good ratings, and not too much traffic on the drive home. If you live in L.A., that means driving north in the morning and south in the evening. If it was the other way, I would've quit after two seasons. Nothing's worse than traffic. I couldn't imagine what my father would've done if he had to drive into the city every day instead of taking the subway. He probably would've killed himself.

The Hardest Part of Creating a Show

TRACY GAMBLE: I would have to say the biggest challenge in creating a show is providing fresh stories and keeping the show real. The easy thing to do is to make it just a purely funny, joke-driven show. I think it is very tough to make a character-driven comedy. Sometimes, you can achieve it because you're lucky enough to have a wonderful and extremely skilled cast. However, it's really tempting and easy to just go for the jokes and nothing more.

BILL LAWRENCE: The hardest part of creating a show from scratch—and this might sound too general—is just doing it. In L.A., there are so many people who will say, "I have a great idea for a TV show." My answer to them is, "Then go write it." I can't remember someone out here who hasn't made that statement. There's also a harsh realization in Hollywood that you become aware of every day: When someone says they have an idea for a show and then they say that it hasn't been done before, they are usually wrong. I can bet that it's already been done. Trust me that at least the idea has been thought of. For instance, if someone said they liked the TV show *Wings,* and they wanted to create a TV show kind of like it, but set in a bus station instead of a little airport, my answer is that it has been written. It may have not been filmed, but it has already been done.

What's really liberating is when you realize that it's not truly about the venue, not about the one-line idea you come up with. It's really about execution. There are so many factors that come into play when you're creating a show, most of which are under your control, and some of which aren't. For example, you have to write a really good script that truly represents your characters. You also have to be incredibly lucky with casting when creating your own show. I really lucked out with the casting of both *Spin City* and *Scrubs.* You can have a great pilot that is poorly cast and it will disappear quickly. On the other hand, a ton of shows get made that don't have great pilots, but the cast offers so much chemistry that it clicks. In that case, you hope that the writing will eventually get better. Also, you have to hope the network puts your show in a good time slot and that they will support you. All of these factors have to align in the heavens.

I think the hardest thing about creating a TV show is accepting initially how much is actually out of your control. All you can do is execute the script to the best of your ability, cast it as well as you can, and then it's pretty much out of your hands.

JONATHAN STARK: The hardest part about creating a show is being the boss. We have to deal directly with the networks and directly with the studio, and most people know that this can put a lot of cooks in the kitchen. As showrunners, we get a lot of notes, and I think most networks and studios agree that a lot of scripts are "over-noted." Because of that factor, you have to be extremely careful and weigh what works and what doesn't work. If it doesn't work, you have to call the network, bite the bullet, and say, "I don't want to do this." Then, they answer, "This is only your show's first year on the air. When you get to your third year and you are a successful comedy, you can do that." I guess at that third-year mark the network will listen to you because you have a track record.

The first year is very hard for a show unless the ratings are through the roof. For instance, the network wanted us to have a 10-year-old boy on our show, mainly because *My Wife and Kids*, the show that was on right before us, had one and was successful. However, we don't want to be *My Wife and Kids*. That show does a good job at being *My Wife and Kids*. We want our show, *According to Jim*, to be different from that. The network felt that our main character, Jim, did not have enough problems. I answered, "I'm not sure about you guys, but I have a wife, a job, and a life and I don't even have an annoying sister-in-law and brother-in-law, and I still have enough drama to draw from." Well, we refused to buckle and, thank God, they didn't call our bluff. They let us do the show the way we conceived it. The network and the studio, to their credit, have supported us in many ways.

BARBARA HALL: The hardest part of creating any show is creating "the world." This is my mandate on any pilot I do. The world of the show has to feel like it pre-existed you. You have to believe that the Girardis on *Joan of Arcadia* were walking around the world before you turned on the TV on Friday nights at eight. That's a very hard illusion to create. It has to do with the cast dynamic and how much you, as a writer, understand the backstory without telling it. Somehow, you just know it. It has to have deep roots. To me, that is the challenge, because you are asking someone to walk into this world and believe that it pre-existed them.

YVETTE LEE BOWSER: The hard part is trying to do different things such as bringing different characters to the screen who aren't necessarily indigenous to the world of the executives that are in the position to greenlight projects. Also, when your point of view and voice is a little different, it's tough to fight for what you believe in. There is a tendency during the development process to oversimplify concepts and to flatten out characters by taking away their truly distinctive attributes. However, I feel characters are not people, they are metaphors for people. So, they have to be more interesting than real people. Also, you have to be clear with your vision and clear with what you want to say, and putting that down on paper isn't always easy. I think that's where the writing gift comes in. When you are creating a show, you have to weed through all that.

SHAWN RYAN: I think the hardest part is coming up with stories that you have not already seen on *CSI, Law & Order, Without a Trace, NYPD Blue, Boomtown, The Wire,* and all of these other police-based shows. I'm not a fan at all of the "ripping from the headlines" style of writing. My attitude is that everybody reads the same headlines in the newspaper, and if you're basing your stories on things like the Scott Peterson case, you know three other shows will be doing the same story as you. At *The Shield,* we start off with the premise that we don't want to take headlines from the newspapers and base shows on them. If we ever do, they have to be obscure cases that nobody has really heard of. So, it's coming up with those fresh ideas and telling them in ways that you've never seen them before that is the primary challenge. We don't always succeed. Nothing annoys me more than us doing a story I think is fresh and then right before we air our episode, seeing the same storyline on another show. We just try our best to tell something different, and it's an ongoing, never-ending challenge. I think we spend a lot more time in the writers' room than most shows do because of our attempt to be different.

The Impact of Ratings and Awards

MARK BRAZILL: I don't look at the ratings every week. It's pretty much beyond one's control. However, I do think scheduling and promotion of the program is a big part of it. *That '70s Show* does okay when it doesn't have *American Idol* with it. However, if it has *American Idol* with it, our show's in the top 10 or 20. But you can't say to yourself, "Look how much better the show is doing." It's the same show. I believe that it's just about scheduling. When I do look at the ratings, I find them interesting. Anybody can spin the ratings results anyway they want. For instance, one can say, "We are in the top 10 of women from 60 to 65!" [Laughing] There is a whole department in the network that analyzes the ratings and all of its variables. You can go nuts paying attention to the ratings.

As far as awards go, *3rd Rock from the Sun* had been nominated for numerous Emmies. I went to the awards because I felt it would be great to have the statue, but the truth is that I'd rather have the show syndicated and running every day.

BRENDA HAMPTON: I call in every Tuesday morning to see what the ratings are. As far as obsessing over them, I do not. What I actually do to see how the audience really feels about my show is to read the fan mail. When I have time on Monday afternoons, I open the mail and I put in calls to the people who sent me telephone numbers. First, I remind them to watch the show that night. If they have a complaint about the show, I listen and talk to them about it. If there is something they particularly liked, I asked them why they liked it. I ask them what they want to see more of. I ask them other important questions, including information about who they are, where they live, who their friends are, and do their friends watch *7th Heaven*? It's a fun process for me. Some of the kids scream and get so nervous when I call that they put their mothers on the phone, instead of talking to me directly. Others kids will stay on the phone. There are some people who I've had a dialogue with for years. However, it's not always positive, because sometimes they are really upset about something. Most of the time, they are just totally surprised that I called. [Laughing] One really positive thing that happened was when a little girl named Sylvia Larosa wrote me a fan letter. It was during the first season. She told me that she watched the show and one day wanted to become either an actress or an executive producer.

However, she didn't know what an executive producer did. So, I called Sylvia up and told her that she could come to my office and I would show her what an executive producer does. We have kept in touch for five years! She is now in college and wants to become a writer. That's especially rewarding for me.

TOM FONTANA: Yes, awards are, in fact, meaningful to me in the sense that it's emotionally great to win an award. However, it has no ultimate value. Awards may have some small degree of value in terms of your next deal, but I actually don't even think they have that. It's not like I sit upstairs with my Emmy Awards and say I'm the best writer in television. I suppose that it goes back to the advice Bruce Paltrow gave me long ago about believing in yourself no matter what others say. However, I will never openly profess that I don't want to win an award. That would be hypocritical. I will fly to Oshkosh to accept an award if I know I'm going to get it. [Laughing] Eventually, though, you recognize the real lack of practical importance that awards have. In itself, that's an extremely liberating thing.

BARBARA HALL: Ratings and winning awards are two entirely different things. I pay a ton of attention to ratings because that is my dialogue with the audience. There are two important things going on with regard to ratings. First, ratings determine if you are going to have a job next year. Secondly, ratings reflect what your audience is saying in response. I am not someone who looks at bad ratings and says I am too smart for the viewer. I don't do that. I just face up to the fact that if the ratings aren't where they should be, then I'm not communicating my idea to this audience. That hasn't really happened to me, because both of my shows, *Judging Amy* and *Joan of Arcadia*, were hits right out of the gate. However, if the ratings start to dip, I would want to know why. I would also take it upon myself to correct that.

As far as awards are concerned, they are great too, but it just depends on the award. For me, though, it's all about the show. I don't get any sort of inner validation by getting an award. It's the show that's being recognized and it means that you're reaching and speaking to somebody and they're speaking back to you. Again, it's all about the show.

ILENE CHAIKEN: I try not to pay attention to ratings because I find that it really does interfere with my ability to just do the work. It just creates too much anxiety. I am always happy to hear that the people to whom ratings are important are getting what they want. It is an important element of what keeps a show going.

It is lovely to be honored with an award, but you always go forward with the knowledge that there are going to be times when people love the work you do and times when it just gets trashed. You can't get too attached to those good moments, because it is not always going to be that way.

JOSH SCHWARTZ: I am only concerned that the show is well received overall and the ratings are solid enough to be able to produce more episodes. When we got an order for 27 more episodes, it was gratifying and also terrifying. That's because it's a lot of hours of television. We were aired after *American Idol* and the powers-that-be had solid confidence in our show. They wanted to run our show without repeats. That was a big vote of confidence as well. It all comes down to whether people are watching. In our case, they are and I'm grateful for it.

LARRY DAVID: I think ratings and awards are very helpful to the show in the eyes of the network and, obviously, if you're single, an award should help you sexually. Winning an award when you're married is sort of a waste. You can't exploit it in any way. It's good for one night and that's it. I guarantee you most single people keep the award in the living room, while most married people keep it someplace where no one ever sees it. I was never caught up in ratings. To tell you the truth, I still don't know what those numbers mean.

TRACY NEWMAN: I don't fully understand the ratings. Nobody has actually explained them to me and I haven't asked. [Laughing] Seriously, Suzanne Bukinik, our partner who comes from the network side, pays attention to the ratings and explains them to me. You need one person around who does that for you.

As far as awards go, the Emmy Award we got for the show *Ellen,* for writing the "Coming Out" episode, was major for our careers. I don't even think I was aware of my body the night we won the Emmy Award. I felt like I was walking on air.

YVETTE LEE BOWSER: When launching a show, I pay pretty close attention to the ratings. When other shows are being launched, I take a look at the ratings as well. I like to pay attention to what the audience wants to watch. Remember, storylines and character arcs are never dictated by numbers. Also, you can't please everyone. If you try to please everyone, you will probably end up pleasing no one and most importantly, you won't please yourself. I'm going to survive or die by my own vision and my own words. I have had a pretty good run and I feel good about what I have done thus far.

SHAWN RYAN: I knew that my Emmy nomination for my writing came about for several reasons—from how good the actors delivered my words, how good the directing was, and how good the crew did in putting this show together. When Michael Chiklis won the Emmy Award for Best Actor in a Drama Series for *The Shield*, I certainly felt he deserved it and that he did an amazing job. When we won a Golden Globe for Best Drama Series, it felt like a real team win. It was a great night in my life. It encourages you to keep moving forward.

AMY SHERMAN-PALLADINO: I feel the Television Academy does not recognize *Gilmore Girls* or any other WB Network show because of what The WB is basically perceived as—a kids' network. Its viewers are considered to be young teens. I think Lauren Graham would have been nominated our first year if we weren't on The WB. She had developed a lot of heat after being nominated for a Golden Globe and a SAG award. The fact that she wasn't nominated for an Emmy Award was unfair, but the Television Academy voters simply do not watch The WB Network. I don't really care, because, in the end, an Emmy Award is a great party and a moment in the sun, but that's not the bottom line. The work I'm allowed to do on *The Gilmore Girls* and the amount of freedom The WB gives me is worth much more to me than receiving awards. If I were offered the freedom to create or to receive an Emmy, I would take that artistic freedom.

Dealing with the Network

TOM FONTANA: I've always felt celebrated at HBO and believe that they loved what I did and encouraged me to do what I believed in. HBO has been wonderful to deal with. To do a series where you don't have to prove every year that you belong on the schedule is a great thing. *Oz* did, in fact, get attention both critically and from the subscribers. I don't think, tonally, it set any kind of standards, because *Oz* is nothing like *The Sopranos*, and *The Sopranos* is nothing like *Six Feet Under*. I think that what *Oz* did accomplish is to say to HBO, "Look, it is definitely okay to trust creative people." You don't have to beat them. You can celebrate them.

DAVE HACKEL: CBS gave me a great opportunity with *Becker*, and I'm very grateful for it. However, let's face it, the networks are in this business to make money. They are not just in this to make television shows. If you, as a viewer, would agree to watch the commercials with no television shows, you would save them a fortune. Remember that it costs a lot of money to produce a television show. If CBS couldn't sell advertising spots during my show, they wouldn't produce my show. I'm very happy that they found a way to make money from *Becker*, because I have had a great time doing it. I feel like I'm the luckiest guy the in the world because I found something that I love to do and somebody has allowed me to do it.

TRACY GAMBLE: ABC and Disney have been very cooperative. For instance, writing the pilot script was my baby. The author, W. Bruce Cameron, tried to have control, but I said, "No, I have a clear vision for this series. Please let me move ahead." Bruce wrote the book, but I was living the book every single day of my life. ABC and Disney were very supportive of my position. In the end, I was able to execute what I thought was a strong pilot script. I brought to the pilot script my own personal experiences of being a real-life Paul Hennessy, and I think that honesty came through in my writing. I think the network as well as my executive producers, Tom Shadyac and Flody Suarez, saw that in my work and supported me.

MAX MUTCHNICK: The first time David and I really dealt directly with a network was when we did our initial pilot for the first show we created, *Boston Common*. David and I knew that once we researched the whole thing, we had the good taste to make the right choices. We left a meeting with the network, and the last thing we said to the head of NBC, Warren Littlefield, was, "Please give us the keys to this car, and if we scratch it, we will give it back. However, just give us the chance to drive it ourselves." NBC refused and told our agent that we were two novices and to get experienced showrunners. Well, our agent knew that we really wanted to do this without interference. So, he basically hired extras to come to the table-read of the pilot of *Boston Common*. They were actually established showrunners who were also our agent's clients, and he asked them to just sit there for the pilot. After the pilot was shot, we never saw them again and we were off and running. When the smoke cleared, we had our own show on NBC, and we learned everything from that experience. The network, especially when you're just starting out in your career, wants to make sure that everything is going to run smoothly because they invest a lot of money in these projects. Naturally, as creators of the project, you want to do it yourselves. So, it is a give-and-take.

SHAWN RYAN: *The Shield* has been good for FX because it has landed the network on the map, critically. FX has been good to *The Shield* in allowing us to write and produce the show that we want to make. FX is certainly building from us, and that's a constructive thing. Their show, *Nip/Tuck,* is doing very well, and they have some other key pilots that they are going to make. Nothing would please me more than to take a look three years down the road and see them airing a solid slate of good shows, with *The Shield* being the grandfather to them all and still sticking around. It's been great to start with a brand-new network. Both of us were working at a low profile, and that it's come this far is really gratifying.

Ending a Show

YVETTE LEE BOWSER: In the case of *Living Single*, the network simply ended it. It was rather unfortunate and an unceremonious ending for a show that meant so much to the network. Over time, the powers that be at a network change, and although you are a "golden child" to one executive, you might not be to the next. I think *Living Single* was really a victim of a regime change at Fox at that time. Again, we were number one in African-American and Latino households, but we were cancelled. If we were number one in Caucasian households, it would have not been cancelled that way.

TOM FONTANA: It's funny, because I never really expected that I would end *Oz*. I sat down and thought about where I wanted the next season to go. In my head, I knew I had the sixth season, but I wasn't sure if I had the seventh. What I didn't want to do was to get to the end of the sixth season and say, "I should have stopped." A show like *Law & Order* can go on forever, because it is what it is and it maintains that continuity extremely well. A show like *Oz* is a real renegade and has this other rhythm going on. It almost becomes a parody of itself. At that point, it becomes something that I don't even want to watch. And if I don't want to watch it, then why would I want to make it?

JOSS WHEDON: I was not very upset ending *Buffy*. I'm not a guy who cries and looks back at things. In my high school, we didn't even have a graduation ceremony. We just left. At the end of *Buffy*, I was totally exhausted and we had to shut down filming one night because I was too tired to go on. That has never happened before. I was exhausted from seven years of telling stories—144 stories to be exact. I knew it was time to stop. I knew it in every fiber of my being. You can love pasta like nothing else, but when you're full, you're full.

DENNIS LEONI: The ending of *Resurrection Blvd.* was a business decision more than anything else. Our numbers were not the problem because we were up 25% from our previous season. Behind Showtime's other programs, *Queer as Folk* and *Soul Food,* we were the network's third highest-rated show. I think that when Viacom was not able to buy Telemundo, it sealed our death warrant. The reason I believe that is because Viacom has a natural outlet for *Soul Food,* which was on the BET Network, which they bought. Showtime had a natural outlet for *The Chris Isaac Show* because it was on MTV, which is also owned by Viacom. Sometimes it, unfortunately, comes down to the business side of things and is not about the quality of the show. We also won a lot of awards, and not just Latino awards. Two years in a row, we won the GLAAD award, which stands for Gay and Lesbian Alliance Against Defamation. We won that award because we did a story about one of the characters coming out of the closet and then dealing with his father. So, I think that the ending of *Resurrection Blvd.* came down to a business decision.

LARRY DAVID: I left *Seinfeld* in 1996, and they went on to do two more seasons. I came back to write the last episode, which got mixed reactions. The problem with finales is that everyone has their own version of what the show should be, which is not the case with a normal episode. But if I had to do it all over again, I'd do the same thing.

Writing Career Choices

TV Writing Vs. Film Writing

DENNIS LEONI: When feature films are good, they are really good. When feature films are bad, I think they are terrible. There is this elitism that exists throughout the business that has to do with television versus film. Obviously, when you write one film, you make more money than you would make working an entire season on a television show.

Most of the movies that get made now are silly teenage things that I do not go and see. Few films are actually made for my demographic. Many films are made for my 17-year-old and 12-year-old children. My kids love them, but I think they are sophomoric. I think the movie industry has pretty much driven off the adult audience. I think that's why DVDs are the bigger revenue base for feature films today. Adults like me stay home and would rather rent it on DVD. There are some films that should be seen on the big screen, and I will still occasionally go to see those types of movies at the theater. It's really frustrating for me. I do think that one of the hardest things to do is to put a TV show on day in and day out. Guys like Steven Bochco are my heroes because I think the show he created, *Hill Street Blues,* is still a benchmark for all television series drama. Today, I also strongly admire David Chase doing *The Sopranos* and Alan Ball doing *Six Feet Under.* When you can put a show on every week and have that show be as good as any little feature film, you have to hand it to that man or woman creator. Not only is he or she doing great work, he or she is doing it every week. I find that very impressive. I think that both mediums, film and television, can have their own individual rewards for a writer.

LARRY DAVID: If you're writing a screenplay on spec, there's definitely less pressure than the rigors of a 22-show TV season. TV really keeps you on your toes. There is a tremendous sense of relief and accomplishment, both in the writing and filming of every episode. You can get an idea and it could be on the air a week or two later. The film process takes a long time, and if it is not successful, it's gone in a flash, and that could be quite a letdown. With my current show, *Curb Your Enthusiasm,* because I am acting in it, I have to write all the shows before we start filming. I don't want to be writing and acting at the same time. I want to feel confident that we have all the shows written so I can just put all my energy into the performing aspect of it.

TRACY NEWMAN: My writing partner, Jonathan [Stark], and I got a job one summer writing a Disney movie. Going from writing 20-minute sitcoms to a 90-minute movie was really hard. We practically killed each other. [Laughing] Both of these forms have elements about them that can become really hard and sometimes become really easy. Well, the latter wasn't the case here. That was my only experience writing a film, and I have to say that I prefer television writing. I'm not saying that I'm opposed to writing more movies, but at this point, I enjoy the process of writing a television script much better.

JOSH SCHWARTZ: Feature film writing is incredibly frustrating. I think right now I have the best job in the world. In television, you get to write something and two weeks later they are shooting it. Two weeks after that, it's on the air. So, it's that kind of more immediate gratification that you do not get in feature-film writing. I think that from my experience of learning early in my career about film writing and how slowly it moves and how frustrating it can be, I tend to appreciate the immediacy and the volume of television even more. We writers are fragile, and film writing can often be discerning. I will absolutely write film scripts again. However, I think you are flexing different muscles in film writing versus television writing.

BRENDA HAMPTON: I'm a television person. I may be interested in film writing some day, but for now, I really do love television. I think television has been more appealing to me because of the immediacy factor of the medium. You shoot a television script right away, whereas in motion pictures, the process takes much longer. However, the writing process on a television pilot can be very tedious, usually going on for months. I can't imagine what it's like for a film writer, because it can take years to get a film made. I think that's the main reason why I have not tried to enter the film industry. Another aspect that I like about television is the challenge of getting 23 scripts out a year. I think that challenge is very stimulating.

BILL LAWRENCE: I may get into motion pictures eventually, but I really do love television. Having dabbled in movies and seeing that it's truly a director's medium is an important realization and a major difference. As a television writer, you are in full control, and that's a great plus. It would be very hard for me to write something, then hand it off and have someone else do whatever they want to it. I don't think I will jump into the movie business until somebody allows me to direct as well as write my own film.

I think that the movie business is a great business for a writer if he or she looks at it like a job. If you don't mind the actual process of writing the script and then giving it to the director and you don't care how it turns out, then the movie business is great for you. You have to have the attitude that, if it turns out great, well then that's fantastic. On the other hand, if it turns out horrible, then it's not my fault. You have to distance yourself in the film business in that way. Hollywood is filled with TV writers who have written movie scripts that they personally thought were good. You read them and they are really funny, but then the movie turns out to be horrible. In movies, the product is out of the writer's control, once the script is delivered.

ILENE CHAIKEN: Film writing and television writing have very different rhythms. Both are gratifying and, in fact, can be equally enjoyable. Depending on what kind of work you do and what your standards are and what your aspirations are for yourself, you can find them in both TV writing and film writing. I know that there are different ways of making movies and different genres. However, for the most part, especially from my experience as a commercial film writer in Hollywood, there is much more contrivance in any movie script than there is in episodic television. You simply have to deliver certain conventions in writing motion picture scripts. Sure, you can deliver them in unconventional ways. You can be as true to character as you want to be, but you do have to deliver something that addresses the conventions of narrative structure. You must provide three acts, or at least certain payoffs, and provide a certain shape to the whole thing. In series television, you can be less constrained by those conventions. You still want to create effective drama. It is just that in series TV, the form calls for different things. The most memorable moments get delivered in different ways.

TRACY GAMBLE: I thought of writing a film script, but right now, I'm too burned out. I have been doing television writing for 20 years. There's enough of a challenge for me in television right now. I also truly love it. Yes, it's a lot of hours and I'm away from my family a lot, but I honestly enjoy it. I have a truly talented writing staff dedicated to making 8 *Simple Rules* great, and it makes me love this television writing process even more.

JOSS WHEDON: I don't watch too much TV. I think you either make it or you watch it. [Laughing] I do think that most of the best writers working in Hollywood are working in television. Why would writers ever work in movies unless they are directing? Working on movies can be a horrible hell where scripts are often torn apart. You're almost forced to have to direct in film so you can protect the work. Then, you can make it as close to your script and original concept, which is all any writer really wants.

YVETTE LEE BOWSER: I have some film ideas, but I also have a family, which includes a husband and two small children. It's difficult to create the time to develop those films. I have a full-time job where I am running a TV show and in charge of 150 people. The day is only 24 hours long and I have a full slate.

Television writing is my first passion. I really enjoy living with the characters over time. There is an additional challenge in building characters that are complex so that people want to see them week-to-week. It's very different from writing a movie where you can just create the most dark, sinister characters and people love to hate them for two hours. In TV, you have to create characters that have a lot of dimension and flaws because you've got to be able to destroy them and redeem them every week. It's a fun challenge for me as a writer.

J.J. ABRAMS: The writer on a film is not regarded the same way as a writer on a television show, because once the film is being made, they don't really need the writer anymore. Television is this ongoing process where the writer is genuinely needed. It is this Darwinian thing where the requirement is that we need ongoing scripts in order to make the show happen. So, there is an awareness of the value of writers, which, unfortunately, is largely absent on feature films.

Drama Vs. Sitcom

BARBARA HALL: I enjoy the writing process of drama. I didn't like the writing process of sitcom. I didn't like to be in a writers' room. By design, you become a writer in order to be in charge of your own universe. You literally are creating a universe and manipulating it. I felt very much like a captive in the sitcom world. The process wasn't me, because I love the part where you are sitting alone with your thoughts. It didn't feel like my style. It is not at all that I don't like comedy. I love comedy. In fact, I have to write comedy because I'm more interested in the comedy aspect than anything else. I just don't like the way sitcoms are written. If you could take a sitcom and set it up so that everyone could go off and write their own stories, I'd write comedy. Unfortunately, that's not how it works.

ALAN BALL: I came to work for *Grace Under Fire*, and a lot of what we were doing was very formulaic TV writing. A lot of what that entails is putting all the subtext in the characters' mouths, then having somebody explain what is happening or having people explain their behavior and feelings, instead of just behaving and feeling. So, a lot of people in the writers' room would say, "How are we going to know he is upset about this?" I would reply, "You just need a certain look on the character's face and you're going to know." Another thing I was taught when I first entered TV writing was to make everyone likeable, and that's boring, boring, boring. The heart of drama is conflict. If you make everyone likeable and you remove all the subtext, then you also remove all of the conflict.

I think I trust my instincts more now. Granted, winning an Oscar for writing *American Beauty* has made other people trust my instincts, too. I honestly don't know if they would have trusted my instincts if that hadn't happened. I am also a lot smarter and I have a lot more experience under my belt.

I'm a person to whom humor is vitally important in my life. I think the ability to laugh at things is a huge survival tool. Also, I believe that we are living in pretty bleak times, to be perfectly honest with you. For instance, we just sort of sit back and watch as we destroy nature in the name of profits. Therefore, I think you have to be able to laugh, and it's a pleasure to bring that to people. There's this notion that drama is the serious art form and humor is not as difficult to create, not as noble, and not as meaningful. I think that's a lot of crap. Personally, I find that the so-called gap between drama and comedy to be sort of artificial, because laughter is just as important as tears, if not more so. I just find it's in keeping with my own natural sensibility. I find it really hard to write something that doesn't have any humor in it, because I just get bored. At the risk of sounding kind of pompous and fascist, I think there's almost a sort of moral prerogative to keep a sense of humor toward what's happening out there in the world and in ourselves.

BRENDA HAMPTON: I do not find doing a drama to be more rewarding than doing a sitcom. I think they are both interesting in their own right. But, I do think it is fun to make people laugh. I'm working on a show right now with actress Kirstie Alley. We are writing it together and it's the first time I've collaborated with an actor or actress on a script. I have to say that I have had a grand time doing it. Kirstie Alley is brilliantly funny and she's an extremely good storyteller. I have been so thrilled with the process. She has been on great sitcoms like *Cheers*. However, I don't think that being on a sitcom makes you a funny person. Kirstie has a genuine gift of humor and is one of the funniest people I've ever met in my life.

JONATHAN STARK: I would like to take a whack at writing a drama. I think that both comedy and drama are equally hard in their own ways. One of the talented women we work with, Jan Nash, was writing half-hour for years. When we got this show together, we called Jan and asked if she wanted to be a part of our team. Jan said she was going to get into the hour-long format. She is now working on *Without a Trace* and loves it. I'm sure drama is difficult. Writing sitcoms is never easy either. Coming up with stories, jokes, and gags is tough, but in the same sense that if you learn to drive a stickshift, you don't think about it anymore when your driving. This same thing happens in writing a comedy because there's a certain technique in doing it that you don't think about anymore after you've been doing it for a while. I think it really comes down to making an honest assessment of your own talents and asking yourself a vital question: If you're writing a sitcom, can you be funny and tell a great story at the same time? If you are writing drama, can you basically just tell a great story? Most importantly you have to ask yourself, "Are you a real writer?" The only way you can figure out that answer is by sitting in front of that blank computer screen and just typing and writing one script after another. Also, don't give your scripts out to your friends for any comments until you think your scripts are good. If you know somebody who's a professional writer, ask him or her to read your script and give you an honest assessment. The thing you have to remember is that when you ask someone for a totally honest assessment, you have to be willing to take the bad comments, too.

SHAWN RYAN: I think dramas have now emerged to become more popular than sitcoms. I think it actually has a lot to do with technological advances.

Back some 25 years ago, it was very difficult to produce a high-quality hour-long drama. Now, with the incorporation of CGI and with editing becoming so much quicker and easier, it enables us as writers to take drama shows farther than we could have ever gone before. You couldn't make a show like *24* or *The Shield* on a weekly basis 25 years ago. If you take a look today, not many dramas are being re-run on cable, maybe with the exception of *The Rockford Files*. The dramas done back in that era were all directed and edited very basically, mainly because they had no choice. In that regard, they really suffered when compared with motion pictures. The best television shows on the air today compare favorably with movies. I think they had many great writers 25 years ago, but, unfortunately, they were held back from going out into the world and shooting something intense and high-tech, like the hour-long drama that I'm doing right now.

Network Vs. Cable TV

BARBARA HALL: I'm in favor of both cable and network broadcasting. I'm for anything good. I like the fact that the market has been broadened with cable. I've always welcomed the idea of working "under the radar" as you do when you are working on a cable television show. I could appreciate going to a cable network and saying, "Okay, I understand that I don't have as much money, but give me total freedom and I will do something great." I like that creative concept. I have not written for cable yet, but I wouldn't say "no" to it. On the other hand, I like the infrastructure of network broadcast television. They know how to market your show. In a weird way, I like trying to "push the envelope." You definitely can't argue with how immense your audience is when your show is on network broadcast television.

One thing that is hugely important to me is that free broadcast television is, in fact, free. When I grew up, we didn't have much money and didn't go to the movies, because we couldn't afford it. My feeling about free broadcast television is that, it is a fact that these TV sets are in people's houses and we have a wonderful opportunity to make something good come out of them.

DENNIS LEONI: I have no preference when comparing cable to network television. I wrote a pilot script for NBC about an International Relief Organization, which everybody seemed to love. However, I think they got scared away because it might have been a little more expensive then they wanted it to be. I would still love to go back to network television to see what I could do. Last year, I pitched a couple of other projects to ABC, CBS, and Fox. Depending on what happens with the newest pilot I've written, *Black and White*, and with the prospective network being Showtime, I would love to go back and pitch some things of mine to the various networks.

SHAWN RYAN: When considering network versus cable TV, it depends on what kind of show I might be writing. In many ways, I have really made my name off of *The Shield*, which is an in-your-face, morally ambiguous cop drama. However, this has not always been the kind of stuff I've written. I started in this business writing sitcoms. What I've really gotten used to is being authentic in my writing and reflecting the world that we are actually living in. The in-your-face attitude and the foul language we use on *The Shield* are required for this show. Now, if I tried to do *The Shield* on CBS-TV, on broadcast television, I would have a major problem. If the next show I decide to do is a family comedy, then

I would not have a problem being on CBS. I don't have a problem censoring myself. However, I do have a problem writing down things that I don't feel are true and authentic for the property I'm creating. It all depends on the necessary tone of the content and where I want the show to go. I have no problem working for a broadcast network. It just depends on what show I'm doing and what challenges that show presents.

ALAN BALL: When *Oh Grow Up* got cancelled, I knew I had two years left on my development deal. I already began to get calls from other networks to create a new show. They would basically be saying, "We have this terrible idea from one of our senior executives, and we think you would be the perfect person to create the show!" Or they would say something like, "We have this lame stand-up comic that we have paid a bunch of money to and have in a development deal. We think you are the perfect person to create a show around him." I just thought that I'd rather shoot myself in the head than do that. So, I went home and partially as a way of having something to balance out the other cancelled show and partially as just a pre-emptive strike before I got sucked back into what I term "network development hell," I wrote the pilot for *Six Feet Under.* I knew that HBO was genuinely interested in that show. I wanted to try a cable network. I didn't really pitch it or talk to HBO about the characters. I just wrote the script, and I'm very happy I gave cable a shot.

TOM FONTANA: Even though I have been with a cable network for a few years, I would go back to working at a broadcast network. It's not one of those Paris things, where I've danced with the can-can girls and now I can't go back to Omaha. [Laughing] I actually think that there are shows that belong on broadcast TV that make no sense whatsoever for cable.

I'm currently developing something for Fox that's a broadcast show, and it does not demand the kind of flexibility that *Oz* demanded. I worked on broadcast television with *St. Elsewhere* and with *Homicide* and we had to fight to get the shows on the air. It wasn't like it was just an especially strong dose of Prozac that we were putting out there. It was really tough stuff. I'm not bad-mouthing broadcast television by any means. But I do think some of the network executives could look beyond this week's ratings. For example, if *Joe Millionaire* gets huge ratings, that unfortunately becomes reality to certain network ears, and that's the only reality that is out there. To me, that's when broadcast television kind of devours itself.

LARRY DAVID: For a network show, we had a lot of latitude on *Seinfeld.* There were, of course, subjects and words that were taboo. On HBO, there are no restrictions of any kind, although I do miss some of my negotiating with the censor at NBC, which was quite erotic. She would tell me she could only let me have three penises and two vaginas. I'd say, "I need three vaginas." She'd say, "I'm sorry, Larry, I can't give you three vaginas." Yes, I miss that.

BRENDA HAMPTON: I'm interested in going wherever they are buying, whether it's network TV or cable. I wrote a pilot with Fanny Flagg after I read her book *Standing in the Rainbow.* I think that she is one of the greatest writers of our time, and I was so thrilled that she would allow me to buy the rights to that book. We wrote the pilot together, but we did not pitch the idea first. We actually wrote it first and then took it to the networks because I was that sure it would sell. All three networks turned us down. I hope somebody re-reads it and decides to do it, because I feel it is one of the best things I've ever written. It's also written by not just me, but by Fanny Flagg, one of America's greatest writers. You think that you bring solid family television written with Fanny Flagg to the marketplace and it'll sell. However, that wasn't the case here. So, once again, I'm interested in anyone who is buying, whether it is cable or network television.

Taking a Writing Job Just for the Paycheck

BILL LAWRENCE: I have, without a doubt, taken writing jobs just for the paycheck during my career. I took a very corporate philosophy in television. What I mean is that, when you go into a company, you don't want to start at the bottom of the totem pole. However, to get wherever you want in your career, whether you are working at IBM, Apple, or wherever, you have to go from job to job to job and do the work and rise through the ranks. When I came out here to Hollywood, I didn't say to myself, "I can't write for *Boy Meets World* because that's beneath me." Nobody's going to turn around and say, "Hey, you get to be a superstar on this new show." I, personally, believe you've got to take whatever gig you can get and make the best of it. One of the best things about TV writing is this: You may end up on a show that you don't love that much, but, in the process, you'll meet 10 other writers. Maybe one or two of them are four or five years ahead of you. The next year may present a new show and a new opportunity that you do like a lot. The decision to hire you is based on how you performed before, what your attitude was on your previous gigs. How helpful you were on that previous show, regardless of the quality of it, is a major factor. I'm a huge believer in doing what you have to do in order to eventually do what you want to. To me, that means doing anything you can to get closer to the goal of pitching your own show.

TRACY GAMBLE: Some years I signed onto projects because, at first, I liked the paycheck. However, in the end, I've gotten something satisfying besides money from every show that I have ever worked on. I was writing on a show called *Daddy Dearest*, where I made friends for life with two very talented writers, Billy Van Zandt and Jane Milmore. They are wonderful people, but that show went away very quickly. I worked on a Lifetime Network show, created by Susan Beavers. It went away quickly as well, but it was a pure pleasure to work with Susan. Sometimes the relationships I make along the way are what make this business worthwhile for me. I was working on a show called *Hudson Street* starring Tony Danza, which I think was a really good show. However, the masses of America didn't tune in. The audience numbers didn't go up. In this case, I grew to like Tony a lot and I think he's terrific. That's the real plus, not just the paycheck.

TRACY NEWMAN: I worked on *The Nanny,* starring Fran Drescher, and I think that I related to the show a little more than my writing partner, Jonathan [Stark], did. After a while, though, it wasn't an easy place for us to work. So, I think we did that job just for the money. I did enjoy working on *Ellen*. I found her really funny and talented. Essentially, I think everyone tends to take a job initially for the paycheck. However, in television, if you really grow to enjoy the show you are working on, you can get a lot out of it besides the paycheck.

ALAN BALL: I did two seasons on *Cybill*, and many writers came and went. I felt that a lot of the work we were doing was disposable. I wanted to leave. I looked at various alternative possibilities, and nothing excited me. Then, at *Cybill,* they offered me a lot of money to stay. I decided that I would stay one more year and bank a lot of money, so then I could take some time off and work on a script that really meant something to me, something that had soul to it.

By working on two sitcoms I didn't believe in, I felt like I had lost my connection, my passion about my work. Like I said earlier, my friends were starting families and I was dedicating my life, up until that point, to my work. All of a sudden, I was in the sad position that in order to get through the day, I had to sort of not fully care about my work. It wasn't a good place for me to be. During that third season of *Cybill*, I went home at night and poured a lot of my frustration into the script for *American Beauty*. It's no accident that the Kevin Spacey character of Lester is a writer who has lost his passion. However, in my movie, it's more that he lost his passion for living. In writing that screenplay, I got back my own passion for writing. The way the whole experience of *American Beauty* came together was a very synchronistic situation. In the wrong hands, it could have been a train-wreck of a movie. The timing in my own life made it just the right project for me.

Who You Know Vs. What You Know

JOSS WHEDON: I do believe that sometimes who you know is more powerful than what you know. I was very fortunate to have someone read and consider my stuff in the beginning because my father was in the business. That is a big first step. However, I didn't get anyone to hire me or take me on as a client simply because my father was in the business.

I admire some producers who really know how to network. They can call and deliver a famous actor or actress for a key cameo part. The only people I know are the people who work for me or used to. I'm not really part of the Hollywood community as a whole. Sometimes, I say to myself, "If I knew so and so, I could say, 'Hey, do you want to do a cameo?'" At times, it's a little frustrating, because I feel I'm in a vacuum. However, it becomes obvious that who you know can only get you so far. Ultimately, I think what you know wins out in the end. It not only keeps you in the game to make it via your talents, but it makes you realize that your work is worthy enough and that fulfills you as an artist.

MARK BRAZILL: It is definitely who you know that gets you the shot, but it's what you know that gets you to stay there. That's exactly how it was with me. I felt that I knew something and I felt I was funny, but if it was not for the Turners, then nothing would have happened for me. Also, if it was not for Dennis Miller giving me my first job, then nothing would have happened for me. That's how it goes. You need somebody to get you in, but you need to deliver once you get in.

YVETTE LEE BOWSER: I certainly think that I've benefited in my career from having built relationships with certain people over time. For example, Dawn Ostroff, who is the president of UPN, knows she can call upon me because we have a great relationship and she knows I can get the job done. I always put my nose to the grindstone and say a prayer. Yes, I got the opportunity to meet Bill Cosby and had the opportunity to work on *A Different World*. However, I proved myself. I did the work. I stayed focused. I don't know how to do it any other way.

There are a lot of people who are successful in this town and who are, in a sense, wearing "the emperor's new clothes." I have seen showrunners who don't know how to structure a story.

I have a genuine passion for what I'm doing. There are a lot of people in Hollywood who would love to be doing it. They have the talent to do it, but those qualities don't meet up with the right opportunity. I have been fortunate in that way. I don't take luck or fortune out of the equation of making it, either.

ILENE CHAIKEN: You can get a lot done in this business based on who you know, while knowing very little. On the other hand, what you know can really, really enhance what you do if you have the drive and the ability to get it done. The what-you-know part of the equation is difficult sometimes because I'm sure that there are a lot of people who are immensely gifted who have just never managed to get their voices heard. It is nice to think that talent will out, but sometimes it does not always work out that way.

BILL LAWRENCE: The who-you-know component of this business is a factor you can't ignore. The one thing that I understand out here is that no one in this business is looking to do you any favors. Meaning, if you use your dad, uncle, friend of the family, or whatever to get in a door, nobody is going to give you a job unless you are ready to work hard and are really good at what you do.

I think it's ultimately about what you know, but you do have to face the fact that you must first find your way "in" out here. That's why I always used to say that there was a certain equation to succeed in TV writing. By that I mean, you definitely have to be beyond a certain level in the talent department. As long as you are above that level, it's all about persistence and patience, which is just finding your way in, whether it's through somebody you know or some other avenue. For me, it was via the agent Howard West. But I didn't just get signed by him. I first sent him a letter and a script, which he sent back unread. I sent him another letter and a script, which Howard West read and said he didn't like. I then sent him another script. I also called him and kept pestering him so I could get in to meet him and speak to him one-on-one. Essentially, I found a way to get in Howard's door without annoying and alienating him.

I feel that there are two traps for aspiring writers to fall into. One is to say, "Hey, I am really connected and I'll be fine." Those people come out and their connections get them in one door. However, if you don't have the goods, you disappear in Hollywood quicker than you would believe. Writers who are here one year who follow that route can easily be gone the next, never to be heard of again. That's simply because there's a constant flux of new 21-year-old men and women coming to town, and they want those jobs. The other trap is to ignore a certain important part of dealing realistically, becoming holier than thou. In other words, one can make the mistake of not considering the person whom you are pitching. Pounding the pavement is fine, but pestering this guy and harassing that guy along the way is the wrong way to go. The people who do that might very well be talented, but end up leaving town five years later, never even getting a job. This happens mainly because they were too unaware to fully appreciate their place in the situation. They must realize that, if decision-makers will take the time to consider what you want to do, you should actually be in front of them and talk directly to them, being totally respectful and thanking them for their help. Then you considerately ask them who else they might recommend talking to, et cetera.

I don't think Hollywood is any different from corporate America in certain respects. Ultimately, no matter where you are working, the basic questions are, "Do I get along with my boss? Do I get along with the people I am working with?" This is just as important in Hollywood as in corporate America and vice versa.

BRENDA HAMPTON: I virtually know no one and I have been in this business since 1988. I still know almost no one. [Laughing] Certainly knowing someone in the business can help. However, if someone you know who is connected in the business helps you with that first step, then sooner or later somebody else is going to read something you have written. It should be good. No, it must be good, with an emphasis on *must*. It's about the material.

DENNIS LEONI: I would say that the majority of success you experience in this business is due to who you know. This is a business based on relationships. I wish I could say that television is about the best projects succeeding. It's not. It's about the deals that get made, and those deals get made because of relationships. That's the sad truth. Let's say you do a hit feature film. Then, suddenly, all the networks come after you to do a TV show with them. Obviously, when you're hot, you're hot. If it were just about "good," television would not look the way it looks. I know that's a cynical point of view, but I believe it's the truth.

So You Want to Write for My Show?

What Do Show Creators Look for in a Writer?

J.J. ABRAMS: I look for writers who have a point of view. I search for someone who I can imagine myself working long hours with in a room together. I enjoy the writing qualities of those people who have the power to make me laugh, cry, or think. I guess it's sort of the obvious combination of ingredients.

Until you actually start working with someone, you don't really know their work habits. For instance, I'm referring to the pace they work at, mood shifts, their quirks, et cetera. It's really kind of a leap of faith. I guess it's looking for the obvious ingredients, but then realizing how special the "obvious" can be.

BARBARA HALL: I look for originality and a point of view in a writer. I always ask to read something original from a potential writer, because I really have lost my ability to determine whether someone has written a good *West Wing* spec script. Sometimes, I will look for somebody who writes a different spec and not the spec of the hour.

I think people listen too much to their agents. You are a writer, for God's sake. You are obligated to go against the grain. So, I don't understand it when people purely listen to the conventional wisdom. I notice stuff that kind of defies convention.

My favorite thing to read is an original spec pilot script because I want to know if someone can create a world. I want to see what they are thinking. It gives me the chance to see what their storytelling ability is like. It's hard to read movie specs because you don't have that much time. However, I will read plays.

I get inundated with spec material, so I want something to stand out, and I want it to reflect someone's point of view. I want to know when I pick up someone's writing why this person wanted to be a writer. The answer can't be, "Because it's fun," or "It is better than a real job." [Laughing] That simply can't be the answer.

JONATHAN STARK: Tracy [Newman] and I both agree that what we look for first is a good spec script. Then we look for someone who's nice and is going to be easy to be around. You work long hours in this business. You're going to be around these people anywhere from 8 to 12 hours a day, five days a week. So, you have to be able to stand working with them for long hours. Therefore, writing funny material, possessing a good story sense, and being easy to take are all key qualities. I want to have a staff that really enjoys each other, respects each other, and supports each other. There are actually writers out there who don't want to do that. We want a writing staff that's not competitive with each other.

MARK BRAZILL: I look for a background as a writer's assistant. That has really turned out well for me. With that writer's assistant background, they pay attention and absolutely understand the process of writing a show. Also, as a comic, one has heard nearly every joke in the world. When you read spec scripts of another show, you are looking for a joke that stems from character as opposed to a joke that is just a joke. You have to create jokes that absolutely come from character in television. *Friends* is such a perfect example of that. Each character has a specific place where their humor comes from. If I read a spec script, I want the writer to truly understand the characters.

ALAN BALL: I am looking for a writer who has his or her own original voice. Both *Six Feet Under* and *American Beauty* are works that I, myself, would like to watch. When I've sat down to create stuff and found that I was interested in it and the piece would keep my own attention, I've been very successful. I've always failed whenever I sat down and said to myself: "What do I think will sell? What do I think people want to buy? What do I think audiences want to see?" Those are vital questions to some decision-makers, but whenever I have done that, I've failed miserably.

I want a writer who writes from his or her gut and writes about things that make you feel something. Think of something that makes you laugh, makes you cry, or makes you angry. Also, you have to have faith in yourself. If you stay true to what you believe in, all of it will shine through when I am reading your work.

TRACY GAMBLE: I think what I look for most in a writer who is just starting out is the ability to write a good, compelling story. The first rule of situation-comedy writing or drama writing for television is that the story has to be interesting. Tons of people can make it funny. However, it is tough to create the foundation, the good basis of a story. *Everybody Loves Raymond* is my favorite situation comedy right now because they do so many interesting things involving Ray Romano's character and Brad Garrett's character. They have a very funny sibling rivalry. The relationship between the father, played by Peter Boyle, and Ray is great, too.

BILL LAWRENCE: Besides being funny on the written page and presenting a good overall script, I look for two main things in a potential writer: The first ingredient is that the writer must be a good person and easy to get along with. That's pretty basic, but extremely important. Television writing is such a collaborative effort that, ultimately, you are hiring someone you will be spending six days a week with, 12 hours a day, in a writing room working together. If the person is not good at interacting with others, then it can become a nightmare. The other thing, which is a little tougher and makes television writing a very specific form of writing, compared to short story and movie writing, is that you must understand that your job isn't to write what you think is funny. Your challenge is to write what the showrunner thinks is funny. Hopefully, in a great situation, those overlap.

You do what you have to, not what you want. One doesn't readily have that mindset in the early jobs one takes. I think one of the biggest mistakes that young writers make is that they write a really funny spec script for a particular show, but doesn't sound like that show's characters. The showrunner is always going to say that you might be great at eventually writing a pilot or your own stuff, but you have to understand that you have to write this stuff now. It's really about learning the voices. It can be compared with writing a play from scratch where you can have people behave and act precisely how you want, while, in contrast, looking at a play that already exists. If you write a sequel to the Eugene O'Neill play *Long Day's Journey Into Night,* the characters have to sound the same and must have the same relationships and the same dynamics. That's a specific requirement for TV writing and something I always look for in the candidate's writing and something I will always look for in their spec scripts. They have to capture the characters. That's a must.

DENNIS LEONI: I like a writer who is inventive. It's wonderful to see a writer who can come up with a different way of looking at something. William Goldman is probably my idol. Look at what he did with the screenplay he wrote for *Butch Cassidy and the Sundance Kid.* Goldman took two classic Western bank-robbers and turned them into these incredible, three-dimensional characters. He gave them a different perspective on life and a sense of humor and all of the things we never thought of bank-robbers having. Goldman did the same thing with his *The Princess Bride* script: He took all of the clichés of a fairly tale set in the mythical kingdom of Florin, updated them, and then turned them on their head. Goldman is just a brilliant, inventive writer.

JOSS WHEDON: What I look for in a writer is the ability to take a cool story idea and find the emotional resonance in it. Nobody does this better than Tim Minear. He pitches a story saying, "Here is a cool story and here is what it really means emotionally." Everybody on my writing staff has that ability. I have had a staff for eight years, and all of these writers have been with me for a while. A lot of writers who I value did get away when my other shows went down, but I was fortunate enough to hold on to a lot of them. I now have seven writers on the staff of *Angel*, and I have really spent a long time building this group.

In general, what I look for is a writer who gives me a premise that piques my interest and then finds and delivers the emotional meaning in it. That's what writing for me is about, period. Give me a premise that makes me say, "Oh, I want to see that!" Then, have the audience find out what it's really like to be attacking zombies or to be a zombie or to be trapped in a submarine or in space or to be getting divorced. Find something in the content that I didn't expect to hear and develop it. If I see an idea that sparks me, followed by something that really fleshes that idea out, then I know I am in the presence of a writer.

LARRY DAVID: When *Seinfeld* was on, new writers got hired by submitting ideas or premises for shows. That was it. No specs. And, of course, good hygiene was of paramount importance.

What Spec Scripts Do I Write?

YVETTE LEE BOWSER: I personally like it when people write original material as opposed to spec scripts. It can be a one-act play or a short story. I don't know how I would write TV if I didn't draw from things that I lived or experienced. However, if you're going to send me a spec script, *Everybody Loves Raymond* is a really good choice because it has very clear characters. The challenge in TV writing, until you create your own show, is to emulate the pre-existing characters to the best of your ability. You can be inventive within that framework. You can still bring your own flavor to a script of an existing show. Just don't write an *Everybody Loves Raymond* spec script with a storyline where the family is climbing a volcano. [Laughing] That would never happen on that show. When writing a spec script, you have to create something that would actually happen on the show.

SHAWN RYAN: To write a good spec script, you really have to know the show you want to write for. If you want to write a spec script for my show, there are certain things one needs to know. First, I think there is a balance to *The Shield* that is sometimes missed in terms of how people tend to cling to the "bad cop" angle of the show. I actually do believe there's a lot of good police work that happens in the show by the other cops and by Vic sometimes. To me, the show succeeds best when there is a moral dilemma that's at the heart of the story. Take the moral dilemma that doesn't have an easy answer—now, that's the path to be on. To me, a writer has succeeded with our show when he or she writes something where Vic Mackey, or some other character on the show, does something that half of your friends think is the right thing to do and half think is the wrong thing to do. Then, you have succeeded in writing a good episode of *The Shield*.

BRENDA HAMPTON: I do not read spec scripts of *7th Heaven*. My basic reasoning is that I feel like I am putting myself in a vulnerable position if I read a spec script of my own show. That's because if we were thinking of any ideas along the line of what is mentioned in that particular spec script, then the potential writer might think that we lifted the idea from their stuff. I will read original ideas if they come through the Spelling Development Department or somebody who is going to protect me, because we are just so vulnerable to people sending in scripts and then claiming their ideas had something to do with my current or future projects.

JONATHAN STARK: I would love to read a *Curb Your Enthusiasm* spec script because I really like that show. I also like to look at spec scripts of *Everybody Loves Raymond*. We can't read *According to Jim* spec scripts because of legal reasons. Someone might also send me a *King of Queens* spec script, and that is fully understandable, because that show has been on for a while. Unfortunately, I have never really watched it, so I don't know it that well. The spec script for me has to be something that I have watched so that I can truly understand and appreciate it.

When a writer gives me a spec script to read and I tell them there is a problem with it, they may answer, "Well, yeah. But, you see, what I am trying to do is..." I then reply, "It's up to you to make the changes because you are the one writing the spec script. You don't have to do anything if you don't want to. However, you asked for my opinion and I'm giving it to you."

The key to a good spec script is, first and foremost, simplicity. Also, you should only write the characters who are the stars of the show. You should never write in your own outside characters unless it is for a couple lines for someone in support, like a storekeeper, et cetera. You should also remember to utilize the specific sets they usually use for the show, because people who are reading this script probably know the show inside out. If you bring in a bunch of outside things, you are not really writing the show. You may write what the writers of the show might ultimately do, but that is not appropriate for a spec.

The point of a spec is to write your episode to be the closest you can be to the basics of the original. Yes, you have to make it funny, but the story has to be there. The reader must perceive the voice of the show. Even in a show like *According to Jim,* which is really just comedy and not rocket science, you still have to keep the characters somewhat organic. To me, that means, if a line is so non-character-driven that it can be uttered by more than one person, then it is not an organic line and it will not work. You want to keep the characters funny but not insane. One thing we learned when we did improv is that if a character becomes insane, you can't believe that character anymore. You try to keep the character on the edge of making the audience laugh, but you don't want to lose the audience by making the character unbelievable.

BILL LAWRENCE: It's dangerous to present someone with a spec script you've written for their own show. Ultimately, the most open-minded person thinks that they write their show better than someone who has never been in their writers' room. Otherwise, I will read just about anything.

No one realizes that when I get someone's script, it is usually one of fifty I received that week. Even though this may sound superficial, my advice is that it better look right. By that, I mean it better not have misspellings and it better look exactly like the shooting draft does of that particular show. The odds are that I know what that other show's shooting draft looks like because I probably have friends who work on it. Also, the first five to ten pages better be funny. It better not start off slow and then get good because, with so many scripts to read, I may not get to the funny part. If it does not start out strong, it is going to get pushed aside.

A lot of people who come out here mistakenly think they'll find a "window." What I mean by that is, let's say Joe Schmo comes out here and says, "Bill, I know your cousin and I want to be a writer." I'll reply, "Hey, great. When you write a script, send it to me and I'll read it." I never say that unless I sincerely will read it. The mistake people make when they do that is that they rush to write something. They hammer it out and they try to get it over to me too quickly. They want that success and that job right now. It is a huge mistake. Without a doubt, when someone does that, you get something that is not that polished and it is not their best effort. It may have misspellings and not look the way it is supposed to. In most cases, it could have been better if they worked on it more.

One further piece of advice is that when you do get the opportunity to have someone who's willing to help you and look at your script, value it. You'll never get another chance to make that first impression with that person again. So, even if it takes a couple weeks or a month longer, just make sure your script is your absolute best effort.

Writer's Block: Fact or Fiction?

TRACY NEWMAN: The nice thing about having a partner is that if one person does not feel like writing, the other usually will. In television, there is no true writer's block because there is no time for it. Frankly, you have to produce and keep producing. The pace of television is too fast for it. If you are in the middle of a production week, you have to just write through the block if you have one. You have to have that script on the table every morning for the actors, the director, and the other crew members. That's the bottom line.

MARK BRAZILL: For me, writer's block has always been fiction. I have never gotten it. I have always been able to suck it up and gut it out. My script may not have been fantastically well-written at the outset, but it was written. If I can just write a full draft, I can fix it. At least I have a full draft to work with. If I write half a draft, that's good, then I do not have anything, because it's incomplete.

JOSH SCHWARTZ: I don't get writer's block because the best part about writing for television is that there is no time to out-think yourself. Feature films move so slowly, almost like a glacier's pace in comparison to TV, that all you can do is sit around and doubt yourself. For me, being a little on the neurotic side as a person, that's a terrible thing. The next thing you know, you throw out the wonderful film script idea you were working on because you may doubt it. In television, the pace moves so much more quickly. There is virtually no time for writer's block in TV. That has been a really good thing for me and my writing process.

BARBARA HALL: Writer's block is an impossibility for me. There is no such thing as writer's block in television because the cameras keep rolling. [Laughing] As a result, everything might not work 100%, but there is no time for the luxury of writer's block.

I am a huge believer in the concept that you simply have to do it. Built into a writer's life is the temptation of the luxury of procrastination. Even when I was just trying to get novels published, I had self-imposed rules about writing every single day. People would call me and say, "Let's go to the movies." I would say, "No, I can't. I have to write." They would always reply, "You don't have to write. You can write later." I would reply, "No, I have to write!" I understood that other people in my life were never going to validate that. It was my job. I missed a lot of parties because I didn't care about the party.

I have friends who complain about their lack of success. Yet, they are going out every night and hanging out, having fun every day. I saw all of my time as writing time. Discipline is everything for a writer. One has to set hours that one works. If you work in a law firm and somebody asks you to go to the beach and you tell them, "No, I have to work," no one will ask why. You have to treat your job as a writer as seriously as that. Writing is a serious business and a serious calling. I take writing very seriously and I require everyone who feels they have that calling to take it seriously too.

DENNIS LEONI: I absolutely get writer's block from time to time. I think that the more money you get paid, the harder it gets to create. I tell people that when the cursor on my computer blinks, it is actually talking to me. It says things to me like, "Okay, Mr. Big Shot writer/producer/showrunner, now what are you going to come up with? They are paying you a lot of money to come up with something, so come on. Let's go!" It makes it even harder to write because this cursor will not shut up. It is talking trash to me. [Laughing] When I write something that I feel is good, then the cursor will shut up for a while. But, soon after, it starts talking to me again, saying, "All right, what's next?" It's always blinking at me and pushing me to come up with something as good or better.

JOSS WHEDON: Yes, writer's block has happened to me. Fortunately, it hasn't happened too much. I recently went through the worst case of writer's block that I've ever gone through. It was entirely based on other problems and certain kinds of pressures I was feeling. Basically, it did not have to do with the work itself.

I very seldom get writer's block, and a lot of that has to do with the fact that I simply do not have the time. There was a point in my career where I tended to fall behind, and I was filming things as I was writing them. I don't do that anymore. I write pretty fast when I finally sit down to write.

I'm an outline fanatic. Using that approach, I have done the hard part and I know that the premise is going to work. I do not sit down at the typewriter until the very last few days of my writing process. Planning is important to me. I play it all out in my head beforehand. I had to write a scene between Buffy and Angel that was very emotional. I could only write in brief stretches because I was crying so hard.

ILENE CHAIKEN: For me, writer's block is fiction. There are some times when I write better than at other times. However, that fear of the blank page does not happen to me. When you are writing a television series, you have to always be capable of spewing words onto a page. Naturally, when I'm not working on a television series and I am writing a movie or trying to think of what I might want to write, there are times when it doesn't come that readily. I do not think of it as writer's block, I just think of it as part of the writing process.

How Important Is Luck?

DAVID KOHAN: To make a successful show, you have to have effort followed by a little luck. The luck for us in the situation of *Will & Grace* was finding our four principle actors. They are all so talented and bring so much dimension and life to our writing. In the hands of lesser talent, who knows what this show would have been like? So, luck can play a very major role in the success of a show.

J.J. ABRAMS: No matter how successful you are as a writer, no matter how much talent you have, no matter how well you write, no matter how much time and work you put into it—all of that needs to be equal to and surpassed by at least 1% of luck. Luck is an important element in the mix for actors, directors, and writers. People may disagree and say that it isn't true. I know a lot of really good writers who don't make a living. I know a lot of "okay" writers who do. My guess is that everyone who has made it and continues to be successful owes at least something to the element of luck. I am not saying there is no hard work or talent involved. What I am saying is that luck is definitely a huge part of the equation.

TRACY NEWMAN: Luck is very important. That phone call from the Steinkellners asking us if we wanted to be staffed as writers on *Cheers* was a great stroke of luck, because it came out of the blue. We had been working very hard, sending our scripts out all over town, but we didn't expect a break of that magnitude so quickly. To start on *Cheers* as a first-time TV writer is like jumping 20 hurdles in one leap. That came about when my partner, Jonathan [Stark], called Cherie Steinkellner because he was looking to get a mutual friend's phone number. His phone call to Cherie was made when they just so happened to be looking for writers for *Cheers*. It was really a fluke. They read our spec script right away and they hired us right away. Do I think we would have wound up being successful anyway? I think it is possible because we were working hard and were a good team. Do I think we would have had such an easy ride? No. But, that one vital phone call was where the element of luck came into play for us.

DENNIS LEONI: I feel that luck plays a very big part in the process. However, I think that to succeed in this business, you also need to have a tremendous amount of tenacity and perseverance. The people who have a great deal of tenacity and perseverance are the ones who will make it. I could have quit

100,000 times, but I just refused to. In fact, I still refuse to. It is easier in my career now, but it's still not easy. It is not like I can walk into a meeting, snap my fingers, and everyone does what I want them to do. However, one cannot simply give up. You have to believe in yourself. If you pound on that door long enough, it will eventually crack, and once it cracks, you have to be ready. Also, you have to meet as many people as you can because you never know where that opportunity will come from. Once again, this business is about relationships. You have to be around the business. So, living in L.A., in my opinion, is the best thing you can do. You have to hang out and you never know when you might get that call for a job opportunity.

Josh Schwartz: I think a lot of it is luck. For me, to get *The O.C.* made and on the air, I had to get lucky in many ways. If Ben McKenzie had been cast as the sixth lead in that UPN show and, therefore, we cast a different Ryan, I don't know if the show would have worked. If Doug Liman didn't come in as the director after McG had to leave, then I don't know if the show would have gone on.

If you are getting lucky, you have to recognize that and be ready and able to execute. It is tough right now. I'm pretty lucky to be caught up in this bubble with this show, but it's hard to get staffed. It is not the Golden Age of Television by any means. Everyone has been talking about what a horrible year this past one was for television. With the economics where they are right now, there is a lot less room for failure.

Joss Whedon: I think luck is involved. I also think that succeeding has a lot to do with serendipity. Yes, the right time and the right place are factors. When I'm fortunate enough to get a gig and somebody puts their faith in me, I will work as hard as I can to justify their decision. I take pride in that. I am also incredibly lucky. With *Buffy,* I had a network, The WB, with no real identity, that was willing to take chances to establish one. After I met with The WB, I called my friend and said, "They were so nice. They respected me and listened to me." He said, "Yeah, they have no idea what they are doing." [Laughing]

The WB let me create a really weird show. If you think about the first season of *Buffy,* it is not a show in full maturity, but it is definitely a show that is bizarre, often dark, and strange. The WB Network never once really questioned me, and I was lucky enough to have them go along with me.

Mark Brazill: Luck is huge! It really is. Succeeding in this business depends a lot on luck. Did you get the right time slot? Was it the right show in the right season?

I have been lucky. However, I have not been lucky during my whole career. I have written on some bad shows. There is nothing worse than writing on a bad show and being there till two or three in the morning, and working. It can make you physically ill. I have two kids, and babies don't care if you work till three a.m. They are going to cry at five a.m., anyway.

I think my experience with *That '70s Show* represents the definition of luck. I feel that way because the odds that your show will go into syndication is 2000 to 1. If you look at how hard it is to go from doing a pilot to becoming a syndicated show, you know you'd better be lucky. Luck is as important as anything that is going to happen to you during your career.

Advice from Female Writers

AMY SHERMAN-PALLADINO: As a woman writer, you have to have thick, thick, thick skin. You can't be a baby. Don't get upset when people do negative things to you because they know you're a woman. The only thing you can do about it is to just be better. Work harder and be better because, in the end, the best script will get noticed. If your writing is too good for someone to ignore, then someone will want that product. Also, you have to fight for your vision and what you believe in.

Hands down, female showrunners do not get the respect or receive the goodwill that a male showrunner gets. It just does not happen. But, that's okay. I'm a big girl and I can take it. You acknowledge it and keep moving forward. Just put on another coat of lipstick and keep walking.

I think that more women have to get more powerful and encourage other women in the industry to be powerful. You have to support other talented women and hire them. That is the only way it is going to change. Many people in the business will refer to a woman who did something or acted a certain way as "crazy." I then say, "You have to define what 'crazy' is." To me, crazy is not someone who has a creative vision and will fight for it.

YVETTE LEE BOWSER: First of all, I hope that my advice would apply to any new writer, man or woman. That advice would include being prepared for a lot of rejection. Many doors will be shut in your face. However, be steadfast in your confidence and know your worth. I think that is the most solid advice I can give. A lot of people, both males and females, approach me and tell me that they want to become writers. I ask them what they have written, and many times they tell me that they haven't written anything. Well, the first key to becoming a writer is writing. It is not just a thing you say that you want to do. You have to just do it. People even say they can't stay up past ten at night to write. They must face reality because that is what it takes sometimes. To truly succeed, you have to be prepared and you have to be dedicated.

TRACY NEWMAN: First, let me say that I'm older than Jonathan [Stark] is and I happen to be a woman and he happens to be a really funny man. So, I would say, first of all, for women writers to use good judgment and team up with as funny a man as possible, and then you have everything. That is a perfect combination. I would also say that persistence probably wins out. You also have to be a pleasant person to work with. For sitcoms, you do have to be funny. If you have a strong story sense, you can get in the door, but to last, you also have to be funny. Having been at The Groundlings improv group for all of those years and exclusively dating comedians for a long time, I have only been around funny men since my early 20s. I am a great appreciator of a good sense of humor. It is the thing that truly turns me on in life.

I don't really know about the arena of drama writing, but I can acknowledge that comedy is a tough field for women. I think women have to be willing to sit back and appreciate all the humor around them. If you really have a good sense of humor, you can appreciate a good sense of humor in others. That's important.

For women or men to succeed as writers when hired on a show, they need to take notes willingly and graciously. This is a business where you are told what to do. It isn't like writing a book, where you are sitting home by yourself. It is a group effort across the board. The executive producers sometimes tell a staff writer, "I know you think this is funny, but I don't want that approach. I want you to write it this way." A male or female writer has to drop their ego and do precisely what the showrunner says. You find out in the first couple of weeks whether a writer is able to do that. If we all fight in the writers' room, it's just a big waste of time.

Yes, women can be successful in this field. That's the good news.

ILENE CHAIKEN: I don't have specific advice for female writers. Women have so much intelligence and insight. I love working with women. I know that women have obstacles that men do not. I also know that, in some cases, it is harder for women to succeed and get what they are after. I don't think that we should ever consider ourselves to be handicapped by the fact that we are women. I think it is an asset. You should just tap into what it is that makes us good, in part because we are women, and bring that forward in the work. If you are writing action, or writing male genres, I think that women bring something to the material that men do not necessarily have. I think that being a woman is an asset.

Male or female, you have to continue to learn and hone your craft. You have to devote a lot of effort to looking at what works for you and how film and television is written. Determine what the conventions are that make it work. It is really, really important to ultimately bust out of conventions, but I think you do have to understand them as a basis for a beginning.

BRENDA HAMPTON: Do not separate yourself from the pack as a "woman writer." I do not think that studios actually care if you are male or female, old or young or anything else. The bottom line is if you can present to the studio that they can make money from you, then you're in. So, do not weigh yourself down by thinking you have a big strike against you because you're a woman. I, personally, have not found that it's hard to make it as a woman. There are so many people, both women and men, who are very talented who cannot get a job writing in television. It is a very difficult field to get into. However, if you truly love writing and are compelled to write, then you have to go for it. You also have to create some kind of opportunity for yourself. You must try to make contacts, so you can meet people and show them your writing capabilities. Making it in this business is a difficult process, no matter how you cut it.

BARBARA HALL: When I started out in this business, there were no women writers. I was often hired as the female voice. That is not true anymore. Today, there are just as many women writers as men writers. The problem involving women writers and what we are now pursuing is the showrunner position. That is the glass ceiling that we are trying to break through right now. That's a whole other process. Like anything else that women have pursued career-wise, you have to take your time and learn everything you can, so when you do get the shot, you won't mess up. With women, it takes twice as long and the margin for error is much, much smaller. You can't afford to mess up.

Here's valid advice for men or women: You have to learn your craft. If you truly want to be a writer, and I don't mean just for television, it encompasses the pursuit of excellence, and you have to understand what that means. In a way, it is about never being satisfied with what you are doing. I always say to people, "If you think that your script is great and you go read Eugene O'Neill and you still think your script is great, then there is something wrong with you." [Laughing] Or, "If you go read a David Mamet play and you still think you are pretty good, there is something wrong with you." Throughout my own career, I would always try to hold myself up to really high standards. Whether or not I ever got there, I had to believe that I was going to get there and surpass the best. I think there is far too much of an atmosphere of, "Oh, this is good enough" or "This is good enough for television." People are not setting the bar high enough for themselves. They'll see a silly romantic comedy and it makes a lot of money and they'll say, "Oh, I can do that." That should not be your approach to writing.

Advice from Male Writers

ALAN BALL: My advice for someone who wants to write for TV is to stay away from the mainstream networks. Look for the cable channels that really want to present something different. Also, don't write a spec script. Write a pilot. If you write something that has your own voice, it will distinguish you from the rest of the pack. Writing for TV is a ridiculously competitive business. So many people want to do it, but very few are actual writers. There are a lot of writers who are good technicians, have learned formulas, and have gone to workshops. That kind of writer can do a good facsimile of what's on TV. However, I would say that if you are a real writer, then you have to write from your heart. I think that is good advice for someone who wants to write for TV who has a voice and a burning desire to communicate something.

If you just want a job, then I would suggest writing a spec script and following all the conventional methods toward getting hired as a staff writer on a show. If that's what will make you happy, then that's fine and there is nothing wrong with that. Sometimes I miss the days when I was just a staff writer and could sit in the back of the room and just crack jokes. I also didn't have to worry if the story worked or if we were over budget. In a lot of ways, I wish that I just remained a staff writer. That was really fun.

MARK BRAZILL: My advice is to write and keep writing. If your spec script didn't get you hired to write on a show this season, then you have to keep writing. That philosophy worked for me during my stand-up comedy career too. If I couldn't get hired on Johnny Carson's *Tonight Show* with the act I did that night, then I better have a new act in a month. There is no conspiracy. You really have to be directly responsible for what's going on in your career.

I feel you should write all of the time. It is also nice to write something that you do not show anybody, a piece of writing that you don't have to sell. That way you do not put any pressure on yourself. It is its own reward. I know that it seems easy for me to say that because I have a writing job and money. However, when I was a car salesman, I used to write poetry. I didn't plan on showing it to anybody. It just made me feel good. That's what I mean.

TOM FONTANA: The best advice I got was from Bruce Paltrow. He told me, "Don't believe them when they tell you how wonderful you are because if you believe them when they tell you that you're wonderful, then you have to believe them when they tell you that you suck. And believe me, they will tell you that you suck." I think it is incredibly important for writers to have a sense of self, a sense of what we each individually do well. I think you have to listen to your heart, listen to your head, and listen to your soul. Also, you need a couple of people around to tell you that your writing is shit when it is. I firmly believe, too, that if you listen to all the people who say "no," you will be defeated. I was fortunate because I didn't listen to the naysayers. There were a lot of them who said to me that I had no talent and I would never make a dent as a writer. If you are lucky, you will find a Bruce Paltrow, but if you don't find a mentor like him, you have to do it on your own. If that's the case, then you have to believe in yourself that much more.

BILL LAWRENCE: In fairly recent history, there was a very weird shift in the evolution of the television writer. Ten or fifteen years ago, I would tell any college buddy who was funny, quick, and personable to get their ass out here because there was money to be made. I can tell you that now it's much more competitive and that the competition is for very few jobs. The TV landscape is really changing. Basically, cable is catching up to the networks. With television in the state it is in now, there is no real reason to come out here unless it's truly what you always wanted to do with your life. If it is, then more power to you, because I think there are ultimately going to be more opportunities for writers than ever before. I just don't think that the get-rich-quick environment is here anymore.

DENNIS LEONI: My advice for Latino writers is not to write just Latino projects. It is very important to be able to write everything. I'm Latino and I worked my way up through the ranks, writing mainstream television. I have written for characters who were doctors, lawyers, cops, all the way up to characters from medieval England on the show *Covington Cross*. I had to do all of that before I ever saw a Latino show that I wrote, produced, and put on the air. The storylines in all scripts are truly universal. You have to be able to write for all races first, before you make them specific to what you ethnically and racially want to do.

DAVE HACKEL: My advice to writers is to just keep writing. You have to keep working at your craft and stay true to your own unique voice. Also, you should write what you want to watch on television. Trust your own good taste. Write characters that you want to see on a weekly basis. An important thing that I think people who are involved tend to forget is that, first and foremost, this is a business. Aspiring show writers often want to come to work just to laugh and have a great time. They seem to forget that there is a lot of financial responsibility and gambling. That is the reason a network wants this or that to happen, and it's vital for an aspiring writer to be aware of that. Whether I agree with a network's reasoning or not, I understand that they have to make money. I work for a multi-national corporation and I had to learn the business side of this because I work for people who are not in it for the laughs. They are directly involved with turning a profit.

I speak at a lot of places and people ask me, "Why isn't television better?" I hate to be a cynic, but I reply, "It is because you don't want it to be." They ask, "What do you mean? I want it to be better." I then say, "No, you don't. You watch a bad show and buy the products they're advertising on it. It is your way of justifying what shows they are sending you on TV. You have the power to turn shows off, and that will ultimately change what's on television." I also tell prospective writers that it involves long, long hours of work. I have worked on some shows where you hit 40 hours of work by lunchtime on Wednesday. In the middle of hours 50 and 60, you forget how lucky you are as a writer. I come home at the end of the day and it's not like I just worked in a coal mine. However, don't kid yourself! Writing on a sitcom is intense work. On the other hand, it can also be a pretty fun job, too. If you have a job where you laugh out loud every single day, you can consider yourself extremely lucky. As far as those famous big gates here at Paramount Studios, I always dreamed of getting past them. When I first moved to L.A. from Ohio, I wanted to know how I could get through those Paramount gates. I wanted to know what went on inside the studio. Could I sneak in? Could I get past the guard? Now, when I drive through the Paramount gates, the guards actually say, "Hi, Dave." I am having a great life.

MAX MUTCHNICK: Here is some important advice for writers who are just starting out in their careers. Once you get hired as a writer, you must also be a good listener. Listen to the writer sitting at the head of the table. You have to learn the language of this craft. Once you learn that language, you can make it work to your advantage. It is very surprising to me how many writers come to our show, sit in the writers' room, and don't truly listen to the voice of the show. Therefore, they never get it right in the script. They don't understand that an episode has to truly build to a good end to be successful.

I trusted my own judgment in a writers' room and I got the biggest ass-whipping of my life. I was working on a show that wasn't going that well. There are many times a showrunner will ask all of the other writers, "What can we do better next time?" No showrunner really wants to hear an answer, but I was just stupid enough to give an answer, which was actually my take on what was wrong with the show. I said to the showrunner, "This show is sophomoric and we need to smarten it up." You have never seen a room bail out so quickly on a young writer. The wonderful writer, John Masius, who has written for top shows like *St. Elsewhere* and then went on to create *Touched by an Angel* and *Providence*, was the only writer who did not roll away. He stayed at the table with me. John was scribbling on his pad of paper. I was thinking he is writing some pearl of wisdom to get me out of this truly uncomfortable situation. John then handed me his notepad, where he had drawn a cartoon of me blowing my own head off.

What Does the Future Hold?

BILL LAWRENCE: What I am hoping to do in the long run is to create movies. I am trying to create a company where I'll still do my own scripts as TV shows and I'll also produce other people's work. I have been out here in Hollywood long enough to come to an important realization. There are many men and women who are very talented writers and have the chops to do their own shows. However, with the TV landscape being so fragmented and so different, it is really hard for people to break in. I feel that through this company of my own, not only can I get some of my friends going with their own TV shows and their own ideas, but I can also start to actively begin taking credit for other people's hard work. [Laughing] Like the people who were nice enough to help me out, I would love to be someone who helps other people get their ideas going. I am hoping I can make that happen in the next few years.

J.J. ABRAMS: I have a couple of ideas for a new show. I also have plans to direct a feature film.

What I love about the medium of television is that you can tell stories, and if you're lucky enough to be on a continuing road with a series, you can keep telling and developing those stories. It's an amazing outlet. I truly feel blessed that I am able to do this. I hope to continue to tell stories that I find compelling, and I hope other people do too.

AMY SHERMAN-PALLADINO: I want to write and direct a feature film in the next couple of years. However, I do want to keep my head in TV. I loved working for *Roseanne*, and I genuinely want sitcoms to come back very strong again. When you work on a good show, it's fun. I am also looking for a network to sell a new sitcom to—a network that will let my show breathe and thrive. Nobody remembers that *Cheers* was a bomb in its first season or that *All in the Family* tested worse than any show in the history of television testing. You need to have time to let a show come into its own. I definitely know when something doesn't work, and I don't need a network executive to call me and tell me that. No one is going to know what works and what doesn't work more quickly than I will. Also, no one is going to want to change it quicker than me. My name is on it and I want to make it good. I'm going to keep creating new shows until the powers-that-be don't let me do it anymore.

YVETTE LEE BOWSER: I would like to write some different things, and I would welcome doing a couple of half-hour shows that are more hybrids. I hope to see more comedies with female leads succeed in the near future. The networks are always changing their agendas. So, as soon as you come up with the right idea for one network, they change their focus. You have to stay fluid.

I would like to keep doing things that challenge me in different ways. I would like to get down a few of my movie ideas on paper. I have also written a few children's stories that I would like to publish. However, for now, I'm staying focused on what I enjoy most, the collaborative and fast-paced medium of episodic television.

ALAN BALL: In the future, I would like to direct a feature film. I would also like to write a big musical. I used to be a composer in college. I wrote music for sketches and really enjoyed it. I also have an interest in writing a novel. I would also love to adopt a child. I think there should always be something that you haven't yet done. When it gets to the point that you have done everything, I think it is time to call it quits.

BRENDA HAMPTON: In the future, I would like to branch out and try some new areas of television writing. I would like to get back into sitcom writing and I would also like to write a novel. At some point, I may feel that the film process is not too overwhelming, and I may like to try that as well. For the moment, I really love writing for TV.

On a personal level, I would like to adopt more children. I have already done so much more than I ever thought I would do in all areas of my life. I never thought I would get this far, and I am sure a lot of other people in this book feel the same way. That is not to say I cannot go further.

JONATHAN STARK: They are trying to sell *According to Jim* into syndication. As most writers and creators will tell you, as a TV show keeps continuing on and its progress is successful, it dawns on you that, "Wow, they could syndicate this!" That's the brass ring. For me, once this show is sold into syndication, I'd stay with it a little longer. Then, I can sit down and write movies and I don't have to worry so much about selling the material. That's my ideal kind of my situation. I do not want to depend on an income while I'm attempting to sell my movies. At that point, I'll be writing stuff I feel I truly want to write and if it doesn't sell, fine. There is always tomorrow and all the possibilities that go with it.

BARBARA HALL: I want to finish out *Joan of Arcadia*. I actually just sold a novel. I have been published before, but this is the first one in a while, so I am very excited about it. I want to keep concentrating on my music. I am in a band called The Enablers and we just finished our second CD. I am starting to play out a lot and getting booked on a lot of gigs. I have even used some of my music on my show.

DENNIS LEONI: I would like to see my pilot script, *Black and White,* on the air. It is a show that is talking about race in America. I would also like to have my feature-film script made, which is entitled *Pistolero.* It is about a Mexican gunfighter and it tells a classic Western story. However, I definitely don't want to be a poster boy for Latino productions. I think that I've proven I can write anything and everything. I would like to go back to the networks and do some shows there that have some redeeming social value. I think that the best writing takes a story that seems like one thing, and then, by the time the story is over, makes the audience realize that it's not about what they thought it was about—it was a lot deeper and is about something much more important. I think that is what great literature is all about. I like to entertain people, but I also enjoy teaching them about something important at the same time.

JOSS WHEDON: I really need to learn to play a musical instrument. I would also love to produce something for Broadway. I'd also like to explore making a musical motion picture, and I even have some ideas about writing a ballet. Then again, I wouldn't mind taking a couple of years off and teaching. There is also that pesky science-fiction novel that one wants to have written. So, there is very little that I don't wish to be doing in the future. I am sort of a wannabe everything.

TOM FONTANA: When Katherine Hepburn was asked in 1971 why she was acting in the movie version of *Trojan Women,* the Euripedes tragedy, she said, "One wants to have done everything." I have to say that is my philosophy, too. So, I am doing a bunch of different things that I am excited about. I am writing a series of short films for HBO—films about civil liberties, or the lack of them, in a post-September 11th world. I believe that Sidney Lumet is going to direct them. I am developing another hour-long show for HBO and I am developing a show for Fox. I want to write a book from an idea that I sold to HarperCollins about the bad Popes in history. I am even talking to DC Comics about writing a Batman comic book. To me, all of it feeds everything else. I often ask myself, "What are the possibilities out there? What else is out there?" You want to keep challenging yourself and surprising yourself. I love what I do.

Index

About the Author

Photographer, Patrick Raccioppi

Steven Priggé was initially introduced to series television when he worked as an assistant on the hit ABC-TV sitcom *Spin City*, starring Michael J. Fox. He is the author of the recently published book *Movie Moguls Speak*, a collection of interviews with some of the most influential movie producers of our time. Priggé also writes freelance articles for such popular magazines as *MovieMaker* and *Written By* (the official magazine of the Writers Guild of America, West). Priggé lives in New York City.